W9-ATJ-759

Your Happy Healthy Pet

Chihuahua

2nd Edition

GET MORE!
Visit www.wiley.com/
go/chihuahua

Elaine Waldorf Gewirtz

Howell
Book House™

This book is printed on acid-free paper.

Copyright © 2006 by Wiley Publishing, Inc., Hoboken, New Jersey. All rights reserved.

Howell Book House
Published by Wiley Publishing, Inc., Hoboken, New Jersey

No part of this publication may be reproduced, stored in a retrieval system or transmitted in any form or by any means, electronic, mechanical, photocopying, recording, scanning or otherwise, except as permitted under Sections 107 or 108 of the 1976 United States Copyright Act, without either the prior written permission of the Publisher, or authorization through payment of the appropriate per-copy fee to the Copyright Clearance Center, 222 Rosewood Drive, Danvers, MA 01923, (978) 750-8400, fax (978) 646-8600, or on the web at www.copyright.com. Requests to the Publisher for permission should be addressed to the Legal Department, Wiley Publishing, Inc., 10475 Crosspoint Blvd., Indianapolis, IN 46256, (317) 572-3447, fax (317) 572-4355, or online at http://www.wiley.com/go/permissions.

Wiley, the Wiley logo, Howell Book House, the Howell Book House logo, Your Happy Healthy Pet, and related trade dress are trademarks or registered trademarks of John Wiley & Sons, Inc. and/or its affiliates in the United States and other countries, and may not be used without written permission. All other trademarks are the property of their respective owners. Wiley Publishing, Inc. is not associated with any product or vendor mentioned in this book.

The publisher and the author make no representations or warranties with respect to the accuracy or completeness of the contents of this work and specifically disclaim all warranties, including without limitation warranties of fitness for a particular purpose. No warranty may be created or extended by sales or promotional materials. The advice and strategies contained herein may not be suitable for every situation. This work is sold with the understanding that the publisher is not engaged in rendering legal, accounting, or other professional services. If professional assistance is required, the services of a competent professional person should be sought. Neither the publisher nor the author shall be liable for damages arising here from. The fact that an organization or Website is referred to in this work as a citation and/or a potential source of further information does not mean that the author or the publisher endorses the information the organization or Website may provide or recommendations it may make. Further, readers should be aware that Internet Websites listed in this work may have changed or disappeared between when this work was written and when it is read.

For general information on our other products and services or to obtain technical support please contact our Customer Care Department within the U.S. at (800) 762-2974, outside the U.S. at (317) 572-3993 or fax (317) 572-4002.

Wiley also publishes its books in a variety of electronic formats. Some content that appears in print may not be available in electronic books. For more information about Wiley products, please visit our web site at www.wiley.com.

Library of Congress Cataloging-in-Publication Data:
Gewirtz, Elaine Waldorf.
   Chihuahua : your happy healthy pet / Elaine Waldorf Gewirtz. —2nd ed.
      p. cm.
   Includes bibliographical references and index.
   ISBN-13 978-0-470-03794-2 (cloth : alk. paper)
   ISBN-10 0-470-03794-6 (cloth : alk. paper)
      1. Chihuahua (Dog breed)   I. Title.
   SF429.C45G49 2006
   636.76—dc22
                                        2006015140

Printed in the United States of America

10 9 8 7 6 5 4 3 2 1

2nd Edition

Book design by Melissa Auciello-Brogan
Cover design by Michael J. Freeland
Illustrations in chapter 9 by Shelley Norris and Karl Brandt
Book production by Wiley Publishing, Inc. Composition Services

About the Author

Elaine Waldorf Gewirtz is the author of *Pugs For Dummies*, *Your Yorkshire Terrier's Life*, *The Dog Sourcebook*, *Dogs*, *The American Pit Bull Terrier* and *Your Happy Healthy Pet: Miniature Schnauzer*. She has also written numerous magazine articles about dogs. She's also a multiple winner of the Dog Writers' Association of America's Maxwell Award for Excellence, and the recipient of the ASPCA Special Writing Award.

Elaine is a member of the Dog Writers' Association of America, the American Society of Journalists and Authors, and the Independent Writers of Southern California. She breeds and shows Dalmatians in conformation and has lived with several breeds all her life.

She shares her home in Westlake Village, California, with her husband, Steve. The couple has four grown children, Sameya, Sara (and husband Ryan), Seth, and Beth-Jo.

About Howell Book House

Since 1961, Howell Book House has been America's premier publisher of pet books. We're dedicated to companion animals and the people who love them, and our books reflect that commitment. Our stable of authors—training experts, veterinarians, breeders, and other authorities—is second to none. And we've won more Maxwell Awards from the Dog Writers Association of America than any other publisher.

As we head toward the half-century mark, we're more committed than ever to providing new and innovative books, along with the classics our readers have grown to love. This year, we're launching several exciting new initiatives, including redesigning the Howell Book House logo and revamping our biggest pet series, Your Happy Healthy Pet™, with bold new covers and updated content. From bringing home a new puppy to competing in advanced equestrian events, Howell has the titles that keep animal lovers coming back again and again.

Contents

Part I: The World of the Chihuahua   **9**

Chapter 1: What Is a Chihuahua?   **11**
A Toy Breed   11
The Ideal Chihuahua   13

Chapter 2: The Chihuahua's History   **18**
Mexican Origins   18
Mediterranean Roots   20
The Chihuahua Comes to the United States   21

Chapter 3: Why Choose a Chihuahua?   **23**
Are You Ready?   23
Why a Chihuahua?   25
Why Not a Chihuahua?   29
Good Watchdogs   33
Chihuahuas and Other Dogs   34

Chapter 4: Choosing Your Chihuahua   **35**
All Your Choices   35
Finding a Puppy   39
Choosing Your Puppy   43
Adopting a Dog   45

Part II: Caring for Your Chihuahua   **47**

Chapter 5: Getting Ready for Your Chihuahua   **48**
Yard Safety   48
Puppy-Proofing Your Home   *50*
Must-Have Supplies   52
Puppy Essentials   *53*
Bringing Your Chi Home   54
Being a Responsible Owner   57

Chapter 6: Feeding Your Chihuahua   **58**
Choosing a Food   58
Reading Dog Food Labels   *61*
When and How Much?   63
Too Many Calories, Not Enough Exercise   65
The Picky Eater   65
Clean Water   67

Chapter 7: Grooming Your Chihuahua   **68**
Why Groom a Smooth?   69
Grooming Supplies   70
Getting Started   71

Brushing Your Chi   71
Trimming Nails   74
Bathing Your Chihuahua   75
Ear Care   77
Dental Hygiene   78
Eye Care   79
External Parasites   80
Making Your Environment Flea Free   *80*

Chapter 8: Keeping Your Chihuahua Healthy   84
Choosing a Veterinarian   84
Preventive Care   88
Chihuahua Health Issues   90
Common Canine Health Problems   94
When to Call the Veterinarian   *96*
How to Make a Canine First-Aid Kit   *99*

Part III: Enjoying Your Chihuahua   103

Chapter 9: Training Your Chihuahua   104
Understanding Builds the Bond   105
Practical Commands for Family Pets   111
Training for Attention   120
Teaching Cooperation   123

Chapter 10: Housetraining Your Chihuahua   124
Your Housetraining Shopping List   124
The First Day   126
Confine Your Pup   128
Watch Your Pup   131
Accidents Happen   132
Scheduling Basics   134

Appendix: Learning More About
Your Chihuahua   137
Some Good Books   137
Magazines   138
Clubs and Registries   139
Web Sites   139

Index   141

Shopping List

You'll need to do a bit of stocking up before you bring your new dog or puppy home. Below is a basic list of some must-have supplies. For more detailed information on the selection of each item below, consult chapter 5. For specific guidance on what grooming tools you'll need, review chapter 7.

- ☐ Stainless steel food dish
- ☐ Stainless steel water dish
- ☐ Dog food
- ☐ Leash
- ☐ Collar
- ☐ Crate
- ☐ Crate bedding

- ☐ Nail clippers
- ☐ Grooming tools
- ☐ Chew toys
- ☐ Toys
- ☐ Flea, tick, and heartworm preventives
- ☐ Toothbrush and toothpaste
- ☐ ID tag or microchipping

There are likely to be a few other items that you're dying to pick up before bringing your dog home. Use the following blanks to note any additional items you'll be shopping for.

- ☐ _____
- ☐ _____
- ☐ _____
- ☐ _____
- ☐ _____
- ☐ _____
- ☐ _____
- ☐ _____
- ☐ _____
- ☐ _____
- ☐ _____

Pet Sitter's Guide

We can be reached at (___)_____-_____ Cell phone (___)_____-_____

We will return on _____ (date) at _____ (approximate time)

Dog's Name _____

Breed, Age, and Sex _____

Spayed or Neutered? _____

Date last heartworm preventive given _____

Date last flea and tick preventive given _____

Important Names and Numbers

Vet's Name _____ Phone (___)___-_____

Address _____

Emergency Vet's Name _____ Phone (___)___-_____

Address _____

Poison Control _____ (or call vet first)

Other individual to contact in case of emergency _____

_____

Care Instructions

In the following three blanks let the sitter know what to feed, how much, and when; when the dog should go out; when to give treats; and when to exercise the dog.

Morning _____

Afternoon _____

Evening _____

Water instructions _____

Exercise instructions _____

Medications needed (dosage and schedule) _____

_____

Any special medical conditions _____

Grooming instructions _____

_____

My dog's favorite playtime activities, quirks, and other tips_____

_____

Part I
The World of the Chihuahua

The Chihuahua

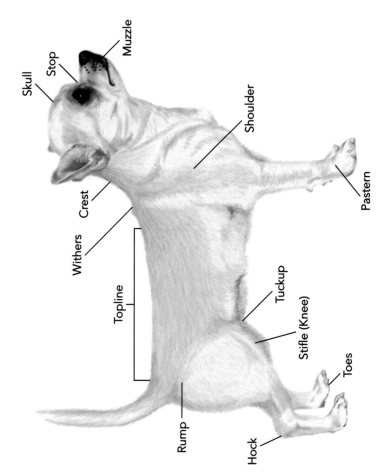

- Skull
- Stop
- Muzzle
- Shoulder
- Crest
- Withers
- Topline
- Pastern
- Tuckup
- Stifle (Knee)
- Toes
- Rump
- Hock

Chapter 1

What Is a Chihuahua?

Ever since the first Chihuahua made his American debut, he's become one popular little Chi muffin. With so much hoopla, it's no surprise that he frequently ranks in the top ten of all dogs registered with the American Kennel Club (AKC).

How is it, then, that a dog who weighs less than a sack of potatoes, has a bony apple head, and spends his time either intimidating intruders or looking for a lap, is so appealing?

It's the cute factor. With this breed it's all about being adorable and affectionate, graceful and alert, swift-moving and compact. And the Chihuahua does it all with a saucy expression that says, "I'm fearless; bite me!"

Here's a breed with presence. Tenacious and tough, you know when a Chihuahua's around because you're no longer in charge. The Chihuahua has no clue that he's smaller than you.

There are other reasons for the Chi's star quality. He needs little grooming, doesn't need much exercise, and once inside your bag, he travels light.

A Toy Breed

The AKC assigns every breed to one of seven groups: Sporting, Hound, Working, Terriers, Toys, Non-Sporting, and Herding. The Chihuahua belongs to the Toy Group.

All breeds in the Toy Group are small, but beyond that, each one has distinguishing traits that set it apart from other toy breeds.

What Is a Breed Standard?

A breed standard is a detailed description of the perfect dog of that breed. Breeders use the standard as a guide in their breeding programs, and judges use it to evaluate the dogs in conformation shows. The standard is written by the national breed club, using guidelines established by the registry that recognizes the breed (such as the AKC or UKC).

The first section of the breed standard gives a brief overview of the breed's history. Then it describes the dog's general appearance and size as an adult. Next is a detailed description of the head and neck, then the back and body, and the front and rear legs. The standard then describes the ideal coat and how the dog should be presented in the show ring. It also lists all acceptable colors, patterns, and markings. Then there's a section on how the dog moves, called *gait*. Finally, there's a general description of the dog's temperament.

Each section also lists characteristics that are considered to be faults or disqualifications in the conformation ring. Superficial faults in appearance are often what distinguish a pet-quality dog from a show- or competition-quality dog. However, some faults affect the way a dog moves or his overall health. And faults in temperament are serious business.

You can read all the AKC breed standards at www.akc.org.

This chapter briefly describes the Chihuahua's breed characteristics, as outlined in the breed standard. To read the official breed standard, refer to the Web sites of the AKC or the Chihuahua Club of America (listed in the appendix).

While car and appliance models change from year to year, breeds remain the same because there is a breed standard. Breeders hope that fifty years from now, a Chihuahua will look very much like the dog you see today.

The standard for the Chihuahua was recorded by the Chihuahua Club of America in 1923. Over the years, there have been changes to the standard, usually for clarification. Even with some slight changes, the Chihuahua has

Chihuahuas are little dogs with big personalities.

remained a relatively stable breed in physical characteristics and has changed very little since his arrival in the United States.

The Ideal Chihuahua

Many dogs are intelligent and have wonderful personalities, but it's the Chihuahua's physical appearance that makes him unique. This is a compact breed with a saucy expression and a terrierlike temperament.

Size

Most Chihuahuas are 6 to 9 inches tall when measured from the ground to the top of the shoulders (the withers), and weigh no more than 6 pounds. Some Chihuahuas are larger than that, and although these dogs can't be shown in breed competition, they are wonderful pets and can be much healthier than the very tiny dogs.

> **CAUTION**
>
> Chihuahuas weighing less than 3 pounds are often called "teacups," "pockets," or "tinies," but these are not another variety of the breed. There is only one designated size of Chihuahua. Some people selling puppies will advertise these little ones as exotic and more valuable, but they're actually just the runts of the litter. Teacups have many health problems and very short life spans.

Coat

Chihuahuas come in coats of many colors and combinations: all one color, marked (white areas on a colored background), or splashed (irregularly patched color on white or white on color). Just a few of the colors are white, peach, lemon, silver-sand, mole, sable, chocolate, blue, red, tan, and fawn. Don't pay more for a supposedly "rare" color, because there is no such thing!

There are two coat varieties, as well: Smooth and Long Coat. Both have the same breed characteristics. Breeders often have Smooth and Long Coat puppies in the same litter, and both types shed.

The Smooth

Smooths have a very short coat that lies close to the body. They may have an undercoat—a layer of soft hair under the top, or outer, coat. The coat may be sparser (approaching baldness) on the chest, the temples of the head, and the ears. The tail has furry hair.

The Smooth should also have a slight ruff around his neck, but no fringes or plume like the Long Coat. If the Smooth Chihuahua doesn't have an undercoat, he won't have a full ruff around the neck and won't have a tail that is heavily coated.

Smooth Chihuahuas are more popular than the Long Coats, and many people don't even know that Long Coats exist.

The Long Coat is soft and full, with fringes along the ears and a ruff around the neck.

The Long Coat

Long Coat Chis have a long, soft, double coat that's either flat or slightly curly, about one to one-and-one-half inches long, with a definite undercoat. The long coat has fringe, sometimes called feathering, around the edges of the ears; a ruff around the neck; wisps of hair extending along the back of each leg; long hair, called pants, at the buttocks; and long, flowing hair, called a plume, on the tail.

The Chihuahua Breed Club

Are you a Chihuahua fan? Want to meet other Chihuahua fanciers? Would you like to learn more about Chi behavior, care, and training? If so, contact the Chihuahua Club of America (CCA), a national breed club formed in 1923 under the auspices of the AKC. The CCA is the parent organization of local Chihuahua clubs throughout the United States.

Members of the national breed club wrote the original breed standard of the Chihuahua, under AKC guidelines, and the CCA maintains it. The CCA holds national dog shows, meets regularly, and disburses information about the breed. Since 1987 it has produced five handbooks containing articles about the breed, facts about the club's history, and information about pedigrees.

A Chihuahua owner can apply for membership in the club and join the network of dedicated Chi breeders and owners who care deeply about maintaining the Chihuahua. For further information, contact the Chihuahua Club of America (listed in the appendix).

Head

This breed's head is his crowning glory and the Chihuahua's most distinguishing characteristic. Chihuahuas have large, well-rounded, "apple dome" skulls. The skull is round like an apple and may have a soft spot, known as a molera, at the top. When you gently rub your hand over the molera, you'll feel a slight indentation. More details about the molera are in chapter 8.

The muzzle, sometimes called the snout, is moderately short and slightly pointed. An excessively short muzzle is not desirable because the teeth may become crowded or breathing problems, including frequent snorting, may result.

The nose is very dark in dark-colored dogs and lighter in light-colored dogs.

Eyes

The Chi's eyes are large, set well apart, radiant, and shiny. They're somewhat full, but not protruding. They should never bulge like the eyes of some of the very short-nosed toy breeds. Although eye color is usually dark, lighter eyes are permissible in light-colored dogs. The ruby eye has a reddish cast to it and is generally found only on very deep red-colored dogs. It's very pretty but is not as common as the dark brown eyes.

Ears

Another distinguishing feature of the Chihuahua's head is his ears. Chi ears are quite large and erect and are set somewhat low on the head. When the ears are at rest, they point to about ten o'clock and two o'clock. When alert, they are carried closer to eleven o'clock and one o'clock, or slightly higher. Ears that are carried as high as twelve o'clock are considered too high and make the dog look rabbitlike.

While a puppy is teething, the ears may be up one day and down the next. Ears are usually fully erect between three and six months of age. If the ears are not standing up by eight months of age, they may never become erect. Erect ears or not, you will still have a very nice pet Chihuahua.

Body

Slightly arched, the Chi's neck slopes gracefully into the shoulders. The body itself is well-balanced. When you measure a Chihuahua from the shoulder to the buttocks, his length is slightly longer than his height. He has a strong, level back, or topline. He also has very dainty feet with well-divided toes.

A Chihuahua should look well-balanced and graceful.

Movement

The Chihuahua moves quickly with strong, sturdy action. Good structure means a healthy dog who can run and play without any restrictions.

Temperament

Fearless, tenacious, and terrierlike, the typical Chi temperament is not fearful, quivering, or cowering. He makes an excellent watchdog, and also likes to entertain his family with his singing ability. If he hears a soprano solo, he'll toss his head back and burst into song. At least, that's what he thinks his yodely, whiny sounds are. But a singing Chihuahua won't win a Grammy any time soon.

Chapter 2

The Chihuahua's History

Scientists believe all dog breeds evolved from only one wild ancestor. Contemporary dog breeds were created and domesticated through selective breeding. People bred to obtain the qualities they desired for certain useful purposes. That's why we have breeds that can track, herd, hunt, guard, and hunt in underground burrows. And that's why there are breeds that are strictly companion animals. The Chihuahua is generally classified as a companion dog, primarily because of her diminutive size, even though she can be trained to do many useful things.

The Chihuahua's ancestry is so steeped in myth, secondhand stories, and controversial history that it is almost impossible to separate fact from fiction. The little that was recorded in bygone days was written in an archaic form of Spanish, making later interpretation difficult. Several theories of the Chihuahua's origin are presented here because all the fables, legends, and stories are fun to read and discuss, even though they may not be true.

Mexican Origins

There are people who insist the Chihuahua is a native Mexican breed because ancient relics of small doglike creatures were found in the archeological remains of the Mayans, the Toltecs, and the Aztecs. The National Museum in Mexico City houses some interesting sculptures. One is of a small dog with large ears, kissing her master. Another sculpture depicts a woman and a child; the woman is carrying a small, erect-eared dog, supposedly a Chihuahua, under one arm. However, Mayan history is very obscure, and some of these early statues bear little or no resemblance to the modern-day Chihuahua.

Toltec Civilization

Sketchy information is available about the Toltec culture, which existed around the ninth century in what is now Mexico. Many believe the modern-day Chihuahua is a direct descendant of a dog called the Techichi, depicted in the stone carvings of the monastery of Huejotzingo. The small dogs pictured there bear a more striking resemblance to our present-day Chihuahua.

According to a theory that first appeared in print in 1904, the Techichi was crossed with a wild breed called the Perro Chihuahueno. This breed originally lived in the wild mountains of Chihuahua, where it foraged on anything edible. The dogs supposedly lived in holes in the ground; had round heads, short pointed noses, large erect ears, slender legs, and long toenails; and were wild and untrainable.

Aztec Culture

The statues from the Aztec era bear an even more striking resemblance to our current dogs. The Aztecs conquered the Toltecs, and their civilization flourished for two centuries, from about 1300 to 1520. A small dog was particularly revered by the Aztecs and became the prized possession of the rich. It is said that these little dogs were so treasured by royalty that some families had several hundred. The little dogs supposedly led a life of luxury and were pampered and cared for by slaves; they were even fed a special diet. During that period, the blue Chihuahua was considered especially sacred. Even today, a blue Chihuahua is unusual.

The little dogs were even buried with their wealthy owners because it was believed that the sins of the

Among the Aztecs, Chihuahuas guided their beloved masters safely through the underworld.

interred would be transmitted to the dog, thus ensuring a safe resting place for the master. It was also believed that the little dog would see her master safely along the journey through the underworld, guiding the deceased through all kinds of dangerous places in the afterlife.

Mediterranean Roots

Some people believe the Chihuahua originated in the Mediterranean region and then became established on the island of Malta. A small dog with the molera trait, found only in the Chihuahua, inhabited that island. From there, the breed was supposed to have been introduced to European countries by sailors in trading ships.

Small dogs resembling Chihuahuas can be found in many paintings by European masters. The most noted work is a fresco painted by Sandro Botticelli, circa 1482, located in the Sistine Chapel. The painting is one of a series depicting the life of Moses and clearly shows a small, round-headed, smooth-coated little dog with long nails, large eyes, and large ears that closely resembles a modern-day Chihuahua. Because this painting was done before Columbus arrived in the New World, it leads one to reconsider the theory that the Chihuahua is a native Mexican dog.

Popular and famous, Chihuahuas are widely beloved today.

What Is the AKC?

The American Kennel Club (AKC) is the oldest and largest pure-bred dog registry in the United States. Its main function is to record the pedigrees of dogs of the breeds it recognizes. While AKC registration papers are a guarantee that a dog is pure-bred, they are absolutely not a guarantee of the quality of the dog—as the AKC itself will tell you.

The AKC makes the rules for all the canine sporting events it sanctions and approves judges for those events. It is also involved in various public education programs and legislative efforts regarding dog ownership. More recently, the AKC has helped establish a foundation to study canine health issues and a program to register microchip numbers for companion animal owners. The AKC has no individual members—its members are national and local breed clubs and clubs dedicated to various competitive sports.

Because of the evidence in these early European paintings, others believe the Chihuahua was introduced to Mexico by the Spanish invaders. However, from the time of the Spanish conquest to the mid-1800s, little is known of the Chihuahua. The Aztec's magnificent civilization was destroyed by the Spanish, along with all information pertaining to the Chihuahua.

With all these theories, you can pick and choose what to believe about the origin of the Chihuahua.

The Chihuahua Comes to the United States

Although it is true that Chihuahua-like remains have been found in some parts of Mexico, the real reason many people believe the Chihuahua is of Mexican origin is because the breed became popular along the border of Mexico and the United States. Americans first became very interested in the breed around the 1850s.

When the breed was introduced to the United States, the dogs were not called Chihuahuas. They were usually referred to as Arizona Dogs or Texas Dogs, because they were often found along the U.S.-Mexican border. Later, many American tourists, fascinated by these tiny animals, purchased the dogs from residents of Mexico, and the dogs became known as Mexican Chihuahuas. Chihuahua is the largest northern state in Mexico, where many remains of small dogs resembling the breed were found. In Mexico, the breed is called Chihuahueno.

In 1888, James Watson bought his first Chihuahua for $3 from a Mexican man. The Chihuahua was extremely tiny and did not survive for more than a year. Sometime later, Watson was able to buy several other Chihuahuas in Arizona, Texas, and Mexico. He spoke of the Chihuahua as being smart and very affectionate. Watson said that unless the dog had a molera in the middle of the top skull, it was not purebred. Basically, the Chihuahuas he described in his writing are recognizable as the Chihuahuas of today.

The first Chihuahua registered with the AKC was named Midget. He was born July 18, 1903, and was owned by H. Raynor of El Paso, Texas. There were five Chihuahuas registered that year.

By 2005, not surprisingly, the Chihuahua was the eleventh most popular dog registered by the AKC, with 23,575 dogs registered. She was the tenth most popular in 2004 with 24,853 registered.

Chapter 3

Why Choose a Chihuahua?

Dogs are amazing creatures. Even when you think you know exactly how a dog might react to a certain situation, he'll surprise you. Perhaps it's because dogs lack the verbal skills that people have and rely instead on cues they take from the environment and by paying very close attention to human body language. Dogs notice every little thing you say and do.

They're born with a sort of canine compass, or some very special skills that guide them throughout their life. These have been refined over generations of breeding to sustain and protect them from danger.

Once you know how dogs view the world, you'll be in a better position to decide if you really want to have a dog. Can you live with a dog, and especially a Chihuahua, who is capable of outsmarting you? Think about it.

Are You Ready?

Are you ready to add a dog to your life? This is a very big decision. The average life span of a Chihuahua is 12 to 17 years, and some have even lived a few years longer. Once you make up your mind to have a dog, he is your responsibility for the rest of his life, regardless of what he does. Your dog will be relying on you to feed, exercise, love, heal, and dress him. Well, clothes are optional, but it's not like he can go out and get a job and hire his own cook, housekeeper, personal trainer, and chauffeur. You are his main squeeze.

When you have a dog, it's practically like having a child because it's a commitment of your time, money, and energy. Hopefully, you're not thinking about getting a dog on the spur of the moment. If so, you'll be living with your impulse for a long time. Thousands of dogs are abandoned every year because their owners no longer want the responsibility.

Give this decision a lot of thought and consider how a dog will change your life. First ask yourself how much experience you have with dogs and if you know how to care for one. If you haven't been the one who is totally responsible before, you'll need to spend time learning what to do—which takes time. You'll need to take your dog to training classes, talk to other dog owners, and read books and magazines about dogs.

Time, Money, Energy

If you have owned a dog before and know the basics, do you have enough time to spend with a dog now? Don't forget that you are the center of your dog's universe and that he needs your attention and affection. Today, many people work long hours and may not feel like playing with a dog, let alone taking him to a training class or out for a walk, or giving him a bath. Plus, there's the cleanup. The Chihuahua may be small but he's just as capable of making a mess and chewing up your best pair of shoes as a larger dog is.

Can you realistically afford to keep a dog? Will his expenses fit within your budget, and do you really want to allocate your discretionary income to caring for a dog? After you pay the breeder or donate to the rescue organization to acquire him, your dog will need bedding, toys, a leash, a collar, grooming tools, and training classes.

If you rent your house or apartment, landlords require extra deposits or cleaning fees if you have a dog. And although a Chihuahua doesn't eat that much, dog food is another expense. Your dog will always need regular veterinary care, plus those middle-of-the-night trips to the emergency clinic, which can be expensive.

What about other family members? Do they want a dog too? If not, there may be disagreements about the dog's care and training, which puts a strain on everyone.

Are there children in your home? If so, you'll always have to supervise your dog when a child is around. You can never predict what either will do, purposely or accidentally, and it's your job to make sure neither is hurt. Will the dog be sharing space with other dogs or animals? If so, there may be issues with everyone getting along.

Certainly, having a dog can be wonderful. Just make sure you're ready and know ahead of time, before you acquire one, what you're getting into. Once you bring a dog home, he's yours for life.

Chihuahuas are very tiny, and that presents a set of challenges that you must be ready to deal with.

Why a Chihuahua?

Intelligent and intuitive, today's Chihuahua refuses to be ignored. With confidence to the max, the Chi takes on an intruder or another dog ten times his size without a moment's hesitation. One look at his piercing marble eyes and there's no question that here's a dog who will keep you on your toes. He'll watch your every step and anticipate your next move. If you sit in his favorite spot on the couch, he'll just nap on your lap.

Exercise isn't high on the Chihuahua's priority list, but if you take him for a walk, he'll enjoy it. Training goes quickly, unless you repeat the lessons too many times. Once he knows what's expected of him, a Chi is bored with repetition unless it's his idea or you praise him for doing it right every time.

Sometimes he enjoys playing with small squeaky toys, sometimes not, and children are iffy unless they're well behaved and know how to act around a Lilliputian leader.

Some people are small-dog people and some are not. Which one are you? To have a satisfying relationship with a Chihuahua, it helps to be a small dog lover. This means being able to appreciate the special gifts this size has to offer and to accept the special needs of minis that you'll always have to be aware of. Why then, are you thinking of getting one?

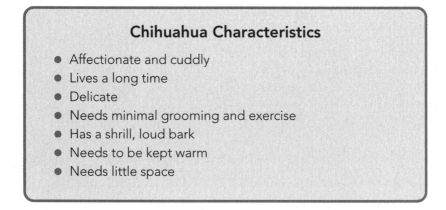

Chihuahua Characteristics

- Affectionate and cuddly
- Lives a long time
- Delicate
- Needs minimal grooming and exercise
- Has a shrill, loud bark
- Needs to be kept warm
- Needs little space

Space Savers

A Chihuahua is ideal for anyone who enjoys living life on the small side. This breed doesn't take up much space inside your home, and, unlike with a big dog, you won't have to worry about him leaping onto the kitchen counter and stealing your sandwich. He won't be jumping up and knocking you over anytime soon. Taking a toy dog for a walk doesn't require a lot of brute strength or athletic endurance, either.

Chihuahuas can handle a variety of climates and living quarters. They adapt well to small homes, but if you live in an apartment or condo, don't assume that you can have pets. In many places dogs aren't allowed, or if they are, the rental agents or co-op board may have strict rules prohibiting dogs from barking and disturbing neighbors. Because the Chihuahua's bark is loud and shrill, this can be a problem, especially if you're late getting home and your dog hears a noise or he's bored.

A dog who weighs less than 5 pounds can squeeze through the gate or slip underfoot without your noticing until it's too late. While it's convenient that a Chihuahua doesn't need much room to be happy, too much room can be hazardous to his health. If there are too many little nooks and crannies around your property, leave it to a Chihuahua to find them and get stuck where you may not be able to find him so easily.

Many Chihuahuas have suffered broken bones after someone accidentally steps on them. Having a toy dog means learning how to shuffle your feet around when you walk so you don't step on him, and always checking to see where your Chi is before turning around.

Low-Maintenance

The Chihuahua is considered a natural dog. He doesn't need his tail docked or his ears cropped. His coat doesn't need to be trimmed, stripped, shaved, or plucked. Bathe and brush him, trim his nails, brush his teeth, and clean his eyes and ears, and he's good to go anywhere. Your Chi is a real wash-and-wear model!

Know ahead that Chihuahuas do shed some. The Long Coats blow (lose much of their fur) twice a year, while the Smooths shed all year round.

A Good Buddy

Chihuahuas can be classified as lap dogs and cuddlers. They enjoy being with you all the time, whether awake or asleep. For every affectionate pat they receive, you'll get double payback in love and loyalty.

Because they are so easy to care for and don't need a lot of exercise, Chihuahuas make great pets for seniors.

Chihuahuas like to be massaged and will often roll over for a belly rub. Use caution when massaging a puppy's ears to avoid damaging the ear cartilage, which will prevent the ears from becoming erect.

The Chihuahua is happiest when he is around people, particularly his owners. He likes to do what you're doing, especially when it comes to sleeping in your bed, but it's not safe to have him in your bed at night. You might accidentally roll over on top of him in the middle of the night.

It's best to train your dog to sleep in his own bed or in a crate. That way, he won't have a chance to steal the covers.

Along for the Ride

Chihuahuas make wonderful traveling companions because they can accompany you practically anywhere. Riding in an airline-approved crate or carry-on bag, they're allowed under your seat in an airplane and they easily fit in just about any car.

Many department stores even let people bring toy dogs with them, but if you're that determined to carry a small dog around with you while shopping, try putting a doggy sweater on a five-pound bag of sugar and carrying that around with you first. It won't take long to realize how sore your arms are! While you can easily drop the bag of sugar off when it gets too heavy, you can't do that with your dog.

Needs Little Exercise

Compared to a dog of 50-plus pounds, a Chihuahua needs very little exercise. He'll get enough of a cardio workout just running around the house. If this isn't enough, he might enjoy trotting around your backyard, and you can always take him out for a walk.

Chihuahuas love to go for short walks, but be prepared for strangers who want to know more about your tiny trotter. Chihuahuas are fast-moving little dogs who are bred to keep up with their owners while walking, but if your dog gets tired, pick him up and carry him the rest of the way home before he becomes physically exhausted.

If jogging is your thing, don't overdo it with your Chihuahua. A two-mile run may be okay for you, but not for your toy dog. A young Chi has little endurance for running, perhaps only a few yards, and he'll need a regular training regiment and conditioning to run much more than that. An older Chihuahua would be able to trot with you over a greater distance, but certainly not more than half a mile. Remember that a human stride of three feet is quite a distance for a tiny dog.

Likes to Play

Playtime with your Chihuahua can be a form of exercise for both of you. A Chihuahua will chase a ball, catch a soft disc, and retrieve small items, but whatever you use for playtime, be sure that your Chihuahua can't swallow it.

Comes in Colors

If you're the kind of person who likes to pick and choose colors, a Chihuahua will fulfill that desire. The breed standard allows Chihuahuas to be any solid color or any combination of colors.

Don't give your dog any stuffed toys that have hard plastic eyes or noses that could fall out and he can swallow, any toys with strings or ribbons that he could choke on, or toys with internal noisemakers that your dog can rip out and swallow. If the toy can fit easily into the Chihuahua's mouth, it's too small and is potentially dangerous for the dog.

Long Lived

You're going to have your Chihuahua for a long time. Their average life span is 12 to 17 years, with some living to 20 years or more! With plenty of quality medical care, the right food, responsible training, and a loving environment, you'll be able to enjoy a long relationship with your Chihuahua.

Why Not a Chihuahua?

A Chihuahua can be a challenge. He's not a passive dog, and not everyone likes a dog who can think for himself and isn't always so willing to please. He has some special needs, too, which have already been mentioned.

Family Dog? Maybe

In an all-adult household, a Chihuahua may be the dog of your dreams. A house full of grownups is usually quiet and orderly, with few loud surprises to startle your Chi. Still, some people complain that a Chihuahua isn't a "man's dog" because of the stereotype that all men like big, rough-and-tumble dogs, while women prefer dogs they can snuggle up to.

But today this is a myth, and Chi fans have come a long way. Chihuahuas have no gender bias, and they will warm up to anyone with a lap. All it takes is a Sunday afternoon, a couch, a big-screen TV, and a football game. Where naps are concerned, Chihuahuas are very good at male bonding and are well known for winning over the men in the household. And once men discover how plucky Chis can be, they're usually hooked on them.

Children are a different story. You would think the tiny Chihuahua would be a perfect fit for a child to hold and cuddle, but that's not always the case. This is a delicate breed who is easily injured, and anyone—adult or child—has to be careful around a Chi. If a toddler loses his balance and accidentally falls on the dog, your dog's back can be broken.

A dog isn't a toy, either. Children don't always know how strong they are, and one hard squeeze will hurt your dog so much that he'll yelp or even bite.

This is why parents must always supervise their children whenever the dog is around and never leave the two alone together. If you have to leave the room, even for a minute, take either the child or the dog with you.

If a child leans over a dog, looks directly into his face at eye level, throws something at him, runs toward him, screams, or grabs him, this is so threatening to a dog that he will act quickly to protect himself. He might growl to warn the child or run away. This should be a clue to your child to leave the

Children are not always aware of how careful they need to be around such a tiny dog. Always supervise your child and your Chihuahua.

dog alone! If the warning is ignored and the dog is cornered, he's likely going to bite. Dog bites are extremely dangerous, often disfiguring or traumatizing a youngster for life. Although it may seem that a dog bites a child for no reason, to a dog's way of thinking, he had every reason to protect himself.

For their own protection, children must be taught early in life what they can and can't do around a dog, and it's the parents' responsibility to watch their children to make sure that they follow the rules. On the other hand, well-behaved children who understand how to treat a Chihuahua may be rewarded with a lifelong companion. It's up to the parents.

Easily Chilled

Finding a place for your Chihuahua to hang around the house is easy. Chis like to be warm. Most love to lie in front of the window when the sun shines directly through it. A Chi also likes to be near the heater in the winter, although this can dry out his coat. (See chapter 6 for information on how to prevent the coat from drying out.)

The Chihuahua particularly likes to be in his own snuggly bed when the air is too cool. One of the ways your Chihuahua will keep warm is to curl up into a ball and tuck his nose under a leg. This gives the dog a pocket of warm air to inhale that helps keep him warm all over.

Some Chihuahuas shiver and shake, which can usually be attributed to fright or a chill. If it's fright from loud noises, unfamiliar surroundings, or previous abusive treatment, obedience classes may help overcome the shaking by building up the dog's confidence.

Chihuahuas get cold easily, so shaking is more likely from a chill. Long Coats seem to be warmer than the Smooths, but if you live where the winters are cold, put a sweater on your Chihuahua if you will be outside for more than five minutes.

Be careful with your Chi on winter walks. Salt, sand, and chemical ice melters are outdoor winter hazards that will play havoc with your dog's feet, so be sure to wash and wipe the Chihuahua's feet when you get home—especially between the toes. A dog can get frostbite and even lose toes, so take care of him in the cold.

Snorting and Snoring

The Chihuahua usually doesn't snore, but occasionally he will. A dog may snore because his muzzle is too short. And sometimes a Chihuahua will snort, which is actually a reverse sneeze. A snort occurs because the dog is so close to the ground that dust gets into his nostrils. To alleviate this problem, make a cup with the palm of your hand and place it gently over your dog's nose without

Chihuahuas are easily chilled, but they don't mind dressing up to stay warm.

The Dog's Senses

The dog's eyes are designed so that he can see well in relative darkness, has excellent peripheral vision, and is very good at tracking moving objects—all skills that are important to a carnivore. Dogs also have good depth perception. Those advantages come at a price, though: Dogs are nearsighted and are slow to change the focus of their vision. It's a myth that dogs are color-blind. However, while they can see some (but not all) colors, their eyes were designed to most clearly perceive subtle shades of gray—an advantage when they are hunting in low light.

Dogs have about six times fewer taste buds on their tongue than humans do. They can taste sweet, sour, bitter, and salty tastes, but with so few taste buds it's likely that their sense of taste is not very refined.

A dog's ears can swivel independently, like radar dishes, to pick up sounds and pinpoint their location. Dogs can locate a sound in $\frac{6}{100}$ of a second and hear sound four times farther away than we can (which is why there is no reason to yell at your dog). They can also hear sounds at far higher pitches than we can.

In their first few days of life, puppies primarily use their sense of touch to navigate their world. Whiskers on the face, above the eyes, and below the jaws are sensitive enough to detect changes in airflow. Dogs also have touch-sensitive nerve endings all over their bodies, including on their paws.

Smell may be a dog's most remarkable sense. Dogs have about 220 million scent receptors in their nose, compared to about 5 million in humans, and a large part of the canine brain is devoted to interpreting scent. Not only can dogs smell scents that are very faint, but they can also accurately distinguish between those scents. In other words, when you smell a pot of spaghetti sauce cooking, your dog probably smells tomatoes and onions and garlic and oregano and whatever else is in the pot.

cutting off his oxygen. Breathing in this pocket of warm air usually stops the snorting. Repeat two or three times, as necessary.

Good Watchdogs

Chihuahuas are excellent watchdogs. Their hearing is acute and their bark is loud and shrill. They have been known to scare burglars and warn owners of fire and other dangers. Because the dog's hearing is so sharp, a Chihuahua will alert the family before anyone in the household is aware of impending disaster. One owner claims that his Chihuahua has always warned him of snakes in his backyard! Another Chihuahua alerted his owner to an intruder entering the house in the middle of the night. The burglar didn't stay long, because the loud and constant barking was a deterrent.

Chihuahuas don't bark any more than many other breeds, and they can be trained to be quiet on command. If you want your dog to protect you, allow him to bark when strangers approach or at unusual situations. But you should discourage excessive and constant barking for no reason.

Chihuahuas won't run up to a visiting houseguest and jump all over the person. They are cautious about accepting a stranger and may continue to bark until you tell them to be quiet. Your Chihuahua will not be aggressive but will

These are vigilant little dogs, and they have a big bark.

Chihuahuas can get along well with other dogs, but supervise carefully when you first introduce them.

look over the guest from a distance, approaching with caution before deciding all is well. The guest should allow the Chihuahua to take the initiative and make the first friendly overtures; this will put the dog more at ease. This doesn't mean your dog is shy—just aware that someone who is not a member of the family is in the house.

With a dog as small as a Chihuahua, the guest shouldn't bend over the dog because the dog may interpret this as a menacing move. Instead, the person should try squatting next to the dog. The next step is to try petting the Chihuahua's chest, neck, shoulder, or back, which is less menacing than reaching for the top of the head.

This cautious awareness of surroundings and people may be due to the Chihuahua's diminutive size. If the dog were to eagerly run up to a guest, the person could scoop up the dog quickly, perhaps dropping or injuring him in some way. If a Chihuahua eagerly accepted strangers, he wouldn't be much of a watchdog, either.

Chihuahuas and Other Dogs

Chihuahuas usually get along well with other breeds, but when a small dog is first introduced into a household that already has a dog, both must be carefully supervised until you're certain they are getting along well.

Many Chihuahua owners have more than one. Two dogs mean more care and training but, in general, double the enjoyment. Also, the two Chihuahuas make good playmates for each other. If you're adding a second dog, choose one of the opposite sex because they will get along better, but they must be spayed and neutered. With multiple dogs, one is always the "top dog" because he's in charge of the other. If two or more Chihuahuas are in residence, each will develop his own distinct personality.

Chapter 4

Choosing Your Chihuahua

If you can't decide whether you want a puppy or an older Chihuahua, just think about choosing chocolate or vanilla. Both ages and flavors are yummy, and each one has advantages and disadvantages. Regardless of which one you choose, your new little Miss Chi will be with you for 12 to 17 years, so learn as much as you can about the behavior, care, and training of puppies and adult dogs before you pick one. Raising a dog is a lifetime commitment, and you want to be sure you can handle it.

Once you decide on either a puppy or an adult and know you can devote what it takes to care for her, the next step is finding the best breeder or a good rescue or shelter organization. Make the right choice now and you'll discover later on that adding a Chihuahua to your household was the best decision you ever made. Maybe you'll even decide to add a second Chi from another source. No one says you have to pick chocolate every time.

All Your Choices

To decide if you want a puppy or an adult Chi, consider how much dog experience, patience, time, and money you have. Each age has different needs that you may or may not want to provide. That's okay. Once you know what those needs are, you can choose the canine companion you really want instead of just taking the first adorable Chi who comes your way.

Once the age question is settled, don't relax just yet. You still have to decide if you want a male or a female, a Smooth or a Long Coat, and the color you prefer (if you have a preference).

Puppy Love

Think you want a puppy? Who doesn't love seeing a cute puppy and all the funny things she does? Probably the person who has to get up in the middle of the night to take her outside to go potty or tell someone that their best pair of leather shoes now has tiny teeth marks. Of course, one little kiss from a Chi baby and all is forgiven—until she needs more attention.

Besides housetraining, crate training, and all the other kinds of training a Chi puppy needs, there's keeping an eye on her 24/7 and a feeding schedule to maintain. Toy puppies must have a meal several times a day for the first few months, plus some exercise and regular outings for socialization. Raising a puppy can be a full-time job, and not everyone is up to the challenge. Plus, it's expensive.

Be prepared to pay several hundred dollars to buy a quality puppy from a reputable breeder. You may think the initial cost of a Chihuahua puppy is expensive, but it's sometimes a lot less than what you'll have to spend on pet supplies.

Puppies certainly have their charms, but they can get into a lot of trouble. Chihuahuas live a long time, and adult dogs can make great pets.

During her first year of life, your Chihuahua puppy will also need to visit the veterinarian a few times for vaccinations (see chapter 8 for more on that). Will you be able to leave work early to take her, and will the cost of these visits fit into your budget? And what about all those supplies you have to buy for her, such as a crate, dog dishes, grooming accessories, shampoo, training classes, a collar, a leash, microchipping, puppy food, and toys? Can you afford these?

Some people prefer having a puppy because they want to do all the training and socializing themselves. They want to build a bond with their dog as early as possible and know that she has a solid start. Or they want to meet the breeder, see their puppy's sire and dam, and the conditions the puppy was raised in, and watch her grow into adulthood.

If you can take all the pros and cons of having a young Chi in stride, then a puppy is definitely the right choice for you.

An Adult Chi

What about an adult Chihuahua? A puppy becomes an adult on her first birthday, so if you choose to acquire an adult Chi she may still be a youngster. Generally though, re-homed Chihuahuas are 4 years old and up.

Whatever her adult age, an older Chi may not be housetrained and may take a little longer to warm up to you. She may also have a few bad habits and you'll have to spend some time retraining her. Plus, you might not know anything about where she originally came from or how she spent her early years.

Many Chihuahuas are abandoned every year for no reason. Others are given up because they have a behavior problem and the owner doesn't want to spend the time or energy to properly train the dog to be a good member of the household.

Happily, there are many older dogs who make great pets and can give you many years of companionship. An older Chi won't need constant supervision and will only require two meals a day, which is an easier schedule to manage. Some older Chi girls may already be housetrained and have good manners. If not, you can always teach an old dog new tricks! Most older dogs have lost interest in chewing things up and are just happy curling up on your lap or going for a short walk, so you don't have to worry about what your dog is doing all the time.

Chances are you won't have to pay very much to adopt an older dog, either. Shelters and rescue organizations usually request a minimal fee or donation, and sometimes the dog is even free.

Perhaps the best part about acquiring an older dog is that you are giving her a home and saving her life.

Male or Female?

A pink or a blue Chi collar? Surely you'll be happy with either sex. Both are sweet and loving, although there are a few differences. The males tend to be more even-tempered, but show no shame about licking their private parts in public or mounting your leg, a guest's leg, or even a throw pillow. They mount to show dominance and may mark their territory by lifting their legs and urinating on anything in or out of the house.

To control your male's enthusiasm, take him to obedience class and establish who's in charge. Watching him closely in the house may prevent him from watering the edge of your couch, but neutering usually stops these bad boy habits.

While some Chi girls will mount, too, if they're dominant, this usually stops once they've been spayed. If a dog isn't spayed it's a hassle. Every five to seven months she'll come in season and have a messy, bloody discharge that lasts for three weeks. She'll do whatever it takes to find a male, even if it means escaping out the front door. The females tend to be moodier than the males and more protective of the house, too.

Smooth or Long Coat?

There are a few differences between the two that you should consider. Smooths seem to be more popular than Long Coats, although that may be because many people aren't aware that longhaired Chis even exist. Many breeders say the Smooths are more outgoing and not as reserved as the Long Coats, and that Smooths are cuddlier. Chihuahuas with long coats often prefer to sit next to you rather than in your lap and can tolerate the cold a little more than the short-haired dogs, who shiver when it even looks chilly.

When choosing between the two coat types, think about how much you mind having dog hair around the house.

When choosing between the two coat types, think about how you like to clean up dog hair: big clumps all at once, or a few tiny hairs sticking into your clothes and furniture all the time? Long Coats blow their coats (lose a lot of hair quickly) twice a year, while the Smooths shed a little all year long.

What Color Is Your Chi?

You've probably seen more fawn-colored Chihuahuas than any other color, because they are the most popular. Both Smooths and Long Coats come in all different color combinations, and all are acceptable in the show ring, but there is no such thing as a rare-colored Chihuahua. If someone wants to sell you a *rare* Chi for a lot of money, don't be taken in. No Chi color is rare.

Chihuahuas can be solid (all one color), marked (white areas on a colored background), or splashed (irregularly patched color on white or white on color). Some of the solid colors you'll see are peach, lemon, silver-sand, mole, sable, chocolate, blue, red, tan, and fawn.

Chis can also have spots or two colors, such as white and gold or chocolate and white. Some reputable breeders may prefer to breed for a certain color or pattern, but many have Chihuahuas in all colors. Whatever color you see on the outside, know that all Chihuahuas are the same little saucy dogs on the inside.

Finding a Puppy

Now that you know you want a puppy and what sex, coat type, and color are your first choices, your next decision is where to look for the Chi of your dreams. Chihuahuas are so popular that you'll see puppies just about everywhere you look: breeders, the Internet, advertisements, pet stores, shelters, and even in a box in front of the supermarket. You may wonder if there's any difference among these. Aren't all Chihuahua puppies the same, no matter where you find them? Hardly! Here are the differences.

Responsible Breeders

Anyone can call themselves a breeder, but not all breeders are created equal. If you're looking for a healthy, even-tempered pet Chihuahua, the best place to go is the home of a responsible breeder.

This person is breeding dogs for the show ring. The breeder is usually a member of the Chihuahua Club of America, a regional Chihuahua club, and maybe a local kennel club. The breeder has dedicated many years to knowing everything about the behavior, care, health, and training of Chihuahuas and gives a lot of thought to selecting a quality sire and dam for every litter bred.

The breeder's goal isn't to sell every puppy in the litter as an extra income. Many responsible breeders even lose money when they breed a litter because they spare no expense in taking care of the mother and all her puppies. The reason they breed is because they want to maintain the quality and health of the breed for future generations. To prove their stock, they exhibit their dogs at AKC dog shows and breed only the best dogs they have.

Going to a responsible show breeder doesn't mean you'll have to buy a show puppy, but that's where the best pet-quality pups will be. Not every puppy in a litter has the conformation or personality to be a show dog, but all the pups in the litter were bred and raised the same way as the top show prospects.

In quality litters like this, one or both of the parents are usually AKC champions and the breeder has tested them and knows they are free from any genetic weaknesses they could pass on to their offspring.

At the breeder's home, you'll be able to see the conditions the pups are raised in, the mother and perhaps the father (or a picture of him), and other relatives such as the puppies' grandparents, aunts or uncles, or half-brothers and sisters.

Responsible breeders prove the quality of their dogs by competing with them. The puppy you get from a breeder will be healthy and ready to face the world.

Observe these relatives; their appearance and behavior will tell you what your Chi puppy will grow up to look and act like.

Before selling any puppy, the breeder screens buyers and chooses the best ones. The breeder has worked too hard breeding the best to just sell them to someone who might not care for them in the long run. Be prepared to discuss your prior experience with a toy dog, how you will train or socialize your Chi, where the dog will be kept, if your yard is secure, and if there are children at home.

No responsible breeder sells puppies to a broker or to a pet store, because the breeder has no way of knowing who the new owners will be or if they can properly care for the puppy forever. The breeder feels permanently responsible for every dog bred and will gladly take a dog back if the owner can't take care of her.

When you go to a responsible breeder you're just not buying a puppy. You're also buying the breeder's expertise. The breeder will answer any questions you ever have about your Chihuahua.

How do you find responsible breeders? The AKC and the Chihuahua Club of America have a network of breeders they can refer you to. Also check with a local kennel club, your veterinarian, and other Chihuahua owners for breeders they recommend.

Chihuahua litters are very small, averaging one to three puppies, so it may be a little difficult to find a puppy. But Chihuahua breeders are always in touch with one another, even cross-country, so someone will know where to find puppies.

Backyard Breeder

Although you'll probably pay less for a backyard-bred puppy, this breeder is breeding for all the wrong reasons. The person may breed a litter because they want to make extra money or so the kids can see a birth. They haven't studied the breed in detail, have no long-term commitment to the future of the breed, and may not have done any health tests on their dogs, so they don't know what genetic diseases their dogs might be passing on to the puppies.

They don't know about pedigrees and will thus breed any male to any female Chihuahua, regardless of their temperament or appearance. One parent may not even be a Chihuahua, may not be AKC-registered, or may hardly resemble what a Chihuahua is supposed to look and act like.

These breeders do not show their dogs, so they're not proving their stock in the show ring and have no incentive to produce the best quality Chihuahuas they possibly can. They don't screen their buyers, either. Anyone with enough money can buy a puppy from a backyard breeder.

Backyard breeders may say they raise their puppies in their own home and treat them like their own children, but let's face it: If someone always has litters year round, how much personal one-on-one time do they really have available to spend with them? Puppies fail to thrive if they're not handled a lot and introduced to many different sights and sounds during their first few weeks of life. These are the Chihuahuas who grow up to be frightened or overly aggressive, and whose owners give up and abandon them years later.

The Internet

Go online to find a puppy and you'll see hundreds of Web sites listing Chihuahua pups for sale. This includes the Chihuahua Club of America, many regional Chihuahua clubs, and responsible show breeders who also offer breed information and have a breeder referral network.

There are many other Web sites owned by puppy brokers and backyard breeders that are very slick and have pictures of puppies available practically year round. How do you tell the difference between the Web sites of responsible show breeders, brokers and commercial breeders, and backyard breeders?

Most commercial and backyard breeders have several different breeds available, and once you give them your credit card number they'll happily ship you a puppy. No questions asked and no health guarantees, either. They may send you a pedigree, but you have no way of knowing who the dogs are that are listed. Often the stock isn't AKC-registered, so you can't prove who the sire really is (the AKC requires all males who sire more than a few litters to be DNA-tested for proof of identity). This is important if a genetic health problem ever turns up in your dog.

If you find a breeder on the Internet who interests you, call and ask them if their dogs are champions and if so, if you can visit their kennel. Buyer beware!

Pet Store

You might think buying a Chihuahua from the friendly clerk at the independent pet store or the retail outlet in the mall is a good idea, especially if they have a return policy. After all, those puppies look healthy and happy. Guess again. Puppies for sale in a store usually come from a broker, a backyard breeder, or a commercial puppy mill—never from a responsible breeder—and you'll be paying a very high price for inferior stock.

As long as your check or credit card is approved, you can buy a puppy at a store. The clerk isn't responsible for the puppy once she leaves the store, and doesn't care about screening buyers to make sure they can properly care for a Chihuahua for the rest of her life. And if the buyers decide a year later that they no longer want the dog, the pet store won't take the dog back.

Often pet store pups are ill when they leave the shop. They may have kennel cough, worms or other intestinal problems, skin problems, or hypoglycemia, but you may not realize this until a day or two later or when you take your dog to your veterinarian for a checkup.

The return policy may have a lot of conditions and doesn't always include a money-back guarantee. If you choose to keep the puppy, you could end up paying thousands of dollars in veterinary bills to restore your dog's health.

You're also getting a pup who is spending the formative weeks of her life in a cage or a storefront window. She is not being socialized carefully and properly. And she is not learning good housetraining habits, either.

Choosing Your Puppy

Take your family with you when you go to pick out your puppy. It's important that everyone agrees on which puppy you choose. Remember that dog ownership is a lifetime family responsibility!

Wherever you find your puppy, try to visit more than once before buying. Get a true feel for the puppy you will be choosing.

Your puppy should be at least 8 weeks of age when you take her home. Some breeders even prefer to keep puppies until they are 12 to 15 weeks to give them extra developmental time with their mothers and siblings. Don't even think of getting a puppy before that time! Puppies separated from their mothers and littermates before the age of 8 weeks may have behavior problems, such as aggression or extreme fear.

Choose a dog who looks bright and outgoing and is eager to meet you.

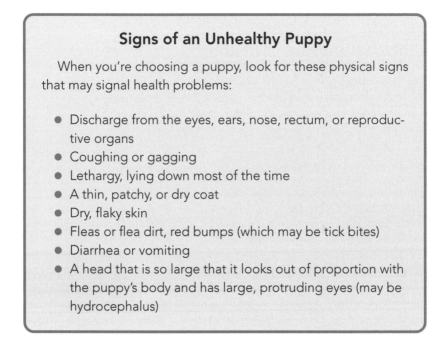

Signs of an Unhealthy Puppy

When you're choosing a puppy, look for these physical signs that may signal health problems:

- Discharge from the eyes, ears, nose, rectum, or reproductive organs
- Coughing or gagging
- Lethargy, lying down most of the time
- A thin, patchy, or dry coat
- Dry, flaky skin
- Fleas or flea dirt, red bumps (which may be tick bites)
- Diarrhea or vomiting
- A head that is so large that it looks out of proportion with the puppy's body and has large, protruding eyes (may be hydrocephalus)

Even though Chihuahua litters are small, look at the whole litter. By watching them play, you can get a glimpse of their individual personalities. Look for a healthy, outgoing puppy who is eager to interact with people and things in her environment. Usually the most outgoing Chihuahua in the litter may be the quietest puppy when she's the only dog and settles into your home. A shy puppy who doesn't run over to you and keeps her tail tightly curled in a downward position against her body may grow up to be fearful around children, so she may not be the best choice for a noisy, busy family.

Don't pick a puppy because you feel sorry for her. A shy puppy may grow into a timid, fearful, and ill-tempered adult. Be certain the puppy doesn't show signs of illness (see the box above). Don't confuse this with tear staining, which is common in Chihuahuas because they have small tear ducts.

> **TIP**
>
> If a puppy has a molera (a small gap in the skull at the top of the head), she requires special care when handling but is otherwise okay. If the molera is larger than a thumbprint or you notice swelling in the area, the puppy needs to see a veterinarian right away.

What's a Teacup or Pocket Chihuahua?

The healthiest Chihuahuas usually weigh more than 3 or 4 pounds. Chis who weigh less than 3 pounds have lifelong health issues. If you want to buy a *teacup* or a *pocket* Chi just because you think the tinier they are, the cuter they are, know that the smaller they are, the sicker they may be.

People who boast that they have teacups for sale who will weigh 1 to 2 pounds as adults cannot predict what a Chi's full-grown size will be. No one can. This is very misleading and is done purposely to attract buyers. Members of the Chihuahua Club of America never use these terms.

If a breeder does have an extremely small Chihuahua pup, it may mean that she isn't fully developed and has heart or lung problems or hydrocephalus.

The Health Guarantee

Responsible show breeders include a health guarantee when they sell a puppy or an adult Chihuahua. Although every breeder's guarantee may be different, most give owners 48 hours to take the Chi to their veterinarian for an exam. If anything is wrong with the puppy during that time, the owner can return her to the breeder for a full refund.

After that time, many breeders may give owners a new puppy if the first one develops any genetic illness within the first two years and she is returned.

When you're puppy shopping, ask every breeder what their health guarantee covers before you buy.

Adopting a Dog

There are many Chihuahuas who need new homes. Go online and you'll find many Chihuahua breed rescue organizations that have dogs who desperately need a good new home. By adopting a rescue Chi, you're giving her another chance to have a good life and you may even save her life.

Part II

Caring for Your Chihuahua

Chapter 5

Getting Ready for Your Chihuahua

Are you ready to cha cha? Your new Chihuahua is coming home soon and you couldn't be any happier. He's an armful of joy, and you can't wait to share your life with him. But before your adventure begins, there are some things you'll need to do that will help your Chi feel right at home.

No matter how old your special little fella is, he needs to have a safe and secure house and yard. Chis are tiny creatures who are master escape artists. They can squeeze themselves into the smallest space possible and find trouble in ten seconds flat. It's your job to Chi-proof your environment and maintain it so that you never have to worry about your Chihuahua.

Yard Safety

Chihuahuas are house dogs who would much rather follow their family from room to room inside than stay out in a yard by themselves. A little outdoor time is okay, but not for hours on end.

Once outdoors, all your Chi really needs is a play space and a spot to relieve himself. A small fenced-in area of your backyard or a dog run will work just fine, but it must be safe and secure without any openings that a tiny dog can slip through.

A pool or a spa in the yard is another hazard if your dog falls in. The best prevention is to keep it securely covered when you're not around or erect a fence with a firmly locked gate.

Poisonous Plants

Check out the plants around your house and yard. Many are poisonous to your dog if he ingests them.

As Chihuahuas reach adulthood, they begin to lose interest in anything other than food and a few toys, but don't relax just yet. Continue to keep a watchful eye on your environment and keep it free from anything harmful to your dog.

After doing all this work to Chi-proof the yard, hopefully your Chi will enjoy going outside for some R&R. Add a comfy pet bed and some interesting toys and he has his own personal resort.

> **TIP**
>
> The Department of Animal Science at Cornell University has an extensive list of poisonous plants at www.ansci.cornell.edu/plants.

Assume your puppy will get into—and under—everything, and make your home as safe as you can before you bring him home.

Puppy-Proofing Your Home

You can prevent much of the destruction puppies can cause and keep your new dog safe by looking at your home and yard from a dog's point of view. Get down on all fours and look around. Do you see loose electrical wires, cords dangling from the blinds, or chewy shoes on the floor? Your pup will see them too!

In the kitchen:

- Put all knives and other utensils away in drawers.
- Get a trash can with a tight-fitting lid.
- Put all household cleaners in cupboards that close securely; consider using childproof latches on the cabinet doors.

In the bathroom:

- Keep all household cleaners, medicines, vitamins, shampoos, bath products, perfumes, makeup, nail polish remover, and other personal products in cupboards that close securely; consider using childproof latches on the cabinet doors.
- Get a trash can with a tight-fitting lid.
- Don't use toilet bowl cleaners that release chemicals into the bowl every time you flush.
- Keep the toilet bowl lid down.
- Throw away potpourri and any solid air fresheners.

In the bedroom:

- Securely put away all potentially dangerous items, including medicines and medicine containers, vitamins and supplements, perfumes, and makeup.
- Put all your jewelry, barrettes, and hairpins in secure boxes.
- Pick up all socks, shoes, and other chewables.

In the rest of the house:

- Tape up or cover electrical cords; consider childproof covers for unused outlets.
- Knot or tie up any dangling cords from curtains, blinds, and the telephone.

- Securely put away all potentially dangerous items, including medicines and medicine containers, vitamins and supplements, cigarettes, cigars, pipes and pipe tobacco, pens, pencils, felt-tip markers, craft and sewing supplies, and laundry products.
- Put all houseplants out of reach.
- Move breakable items off low tables and shelves.
- Pick up all chewable items, including television and electronics remote controls, cell phones, shoes, socks, slippers and sandals, food, dishes, cups and utensils, toys, books and magazines, and anything else that can be chewed on.

In the garage:

- Store all gardening supplies and pool chemicals out of reach of the dog.
- Store all antifreeze, oil, and other car fluids securely, and clean up any spills by hosing them down for at least ten minutes.
- Put all dangerous substances on high shelves or in cupboards that close securely; consider using childproof latches on the cabinet doors.
- Pick up and put away all tools.
- Sweep the floor for nails and other small, sharp items.

In the yard:

- Put the gardening tools away after each use.
- Make sure the kids put away their toys when they're finished playing.
- Keep the pool covered or otherwise restrict your pup's access to it when you're not there to supervise.
- Secure the cords on backyard lights and other appliances.
- Inspect your fence thoroughly. If there are any gaps or holes in the fence, fix them.
- Make sure you have no toxic plants in the yard.

Must-Have Supplies

Walk into any pet supply store or go online and you'll find more stuff to buy for your dog than you ever imagined. The American Pet Products Manufacturers Association (APPMA) reports that the sales of pet supplies and medicine have doubled since 1994. In 2004, pet owners in the United States spent $8.8 billion on pet supplies and medicine.

While everything cute and tiny is appealing, there are only a few things your Chi *must* have when you bring him home. You'll find a list of puppy essentials on page 53. Here are some things to consider when you go shopping for these items.

The Collar

You will need an inexpensive collar and leash for your new Chihuahua on his first day home. Ask your dog's breeder or rescue coordinator what size collar to buy for your dog before you pick him up. Or carry your dog into a pet supply store on the way home and try a few on, so you know what fits. There are so many types of collars that you may have a hard time choosing just one. Don't worry. If you're bringing home a puppy, you'll be buying several different size collars as he grows.

Every dog needs a collar and a leash. For the right fit, you should be able to comfortably fit two fingers between your dog's collar and his neck.

The Leash

One sturdy, four-foot leather leash is all you'll ever need throughout your dog's life, especially if you keep it out of your dog's mouth! Even if your Chi is a total house dog, he'll appreciate going for a walk on a leash.

Never take your Chihuahua outside without a leash attached to his collar. It's illegal to let your dog run loose, and it's very dangerous. A go-getter, your Chi will take on a big dog (and lose) in a flash. Or he'll run across the street because he's curious and be hit by a car.

Do not buy or use a retractable leash! While it looks like a good idea

Puppy Essentials

You'll need to go shopping *before* you bring your puppy home. There are many, many adorable and tempting items at pet supply stores, but these are the basics.

- **Food and water dishes.** Look for bowls that are wide and low or weighted in the bottom so they will be harder to tip over. Stainless steel bowls are a good choice because they are easy to clean (plastic never gets completely clean) and almost impossible to break. Avoid bowls that place the food and water side by side in one unit—it's too easy for your dog to get his water dirty that way.
- **Leash.** A four-foot leather leash will be easy on your hands and very strong.
- **Collar.** Start with a nylon buckle collar. For a perfect fit, you should be able to insert two fingers between the collar and your pup's neck. Your dog will need larger collars as he grows up.
- **Crate.** Choose a sturdy crate that is easy to clean and large enough for your puppy to stand up, turn around, and lie down in.
- **Nail cutters.** Get a good, sharp pair that is the appropriate size for the nails you will be cutting. Your dog's breeder or veterinarian can give you some guidance here.
- **Grooming tools.** Different kinds of dogs need different kinds of grooming tools. See chapter 7 for advice on what to buy.
- **Chew toys.** Dogs *must* chew, especially puppies. Make sure you get things that won't break or crumble off in little bits, which the dog can choke on. Very hard plastic bones are a good choice. Dogs love rawhide bones, too, but pieces of the rawhide can get caught in your dog's throat, so they should only be allowed when you are there to supervise.
- **Toys.** Watch for sharp edges and unsafe items such as plastic eyes that can be swallowed. Many toys come with squeakers, which dogs can also tear out and swallow. All dogs will eventually destroy their toys; as each toy is torn apart, replace it with a new one.

because it gives your dog more freedom to move around outdoors, it can also be responsible for your dog's death. If your Chi is ten feet away from you and a big dog approaches, it will take too long to retract the leash in time to protect him. And if you snap it back too quickly, it can injure your dog's neck.

Toys

Provide your Chihuahua puppy with plenty of safe toys to keep him active and stimulated. Make sure toys do not have small parts that can be bitten off. If the stuffing comes out of stuffed toys, throw them away immediately. Cloth toys should be washable. Pieces of string or ribbon from packages are not suitable playthings for your Chihuahua.

Do not give your Chihuahua old shoes or socks to play with. He will not know the difference between old and new shoes, and it could encourage bad behavior. You do not want to arrive home to find your best shoes torn to shreds. The same holds true for any personal item of clothing or other personal belongings.

Suitable toys include hard nylon bones, which are great for chewing and gnawing. They will keep your Chihuahua entertained and keep his teeth free of tartar. Another good toy for healthy teeth is a rope toy, made of thick rope tied at each end. Toys that encourage you to interact with your dog are also a great idea. Balls and toys of all kinds can turn into retrievable items you and your pet can enjoy together.

Your Puppy's Crate

There are several types of crates available. The hard or soft-sided models should be used only in the winter, because there's not enough ventilation to allow cool air to circulate when the weather is warm. When the temperature climbs to around 78 degrees, use a wire crate because it's much cooler for your Chi.

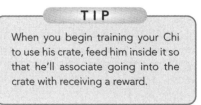

TIP

When you begin training your Chi to use his crate, feed him inside it so that he'll associate going into the crate with receiving a reward.

If the air conditioner is on, cover the top of the crate so your dog doesn't catch a chill. To use your wire crate year-round, purchase a fitted, insulated cover that has a "window" for your Chihuahua to look through and an open area for ventilation.

Plan on taking your Chi on a plane trip with you sometime? If so, consider buying a doggy carry-on bag or hard-sided crate that is airline-approved. These are the only kinds the airlines will allow.

Bringing Your Chi Home

When the big day comes to pick up your dog or puppy, choose a time early in the morning on a weekend, or set aside one or two days during the week when you can stay home with your new Chi. This gives you and your Chi plenty of

A sturdy crate will be invaluable for housetraining and traveling.

time to become acquainted with one another and gives your dog a chance to sniff out his new digs and settle in a little before bedtime. If you're getting a puppy, he should be at least 8 weeks old when you pick him up.

Give your new fella the freedom to run around in a room where you don't have to worry about the carpeting if he has an accident. Introduce him to the rest of the family members one by one. Don't overwhelm him with a big, noisy crowd all at once. His bed or crate should also be in this room, along with a water dish, papers for housetraining, and some new toys.

The First Night

For puppies, the first night in a new home can be scary. Move the crate to your bedroom so he knows you're close by and you haven't abandoned him. If you have a blanket or article of clothing from his previous home, put that inside the crate with another blanket and some toys to help him feel comfortable. Adding a stuffed animal or two will remind him of his littermates and give him something soft and furry to cuddle up against.

This is the first time your little fella is away from his mother and littermates, and he may feel very lonely. Expect some whining or crying, but resist the urge to pick him up because he will think you are rewarding him for this behavior. Instead, speak to him softly and he'll likely quiet down and sleep for several hours.

Picking Up a Chihuahua

To protect your new Chihuahua from injury, teach everyone in the family, including children, how to pick up and hold the dog correctly.

Do

- Place one hand under his chest and the other hand at the rear hindquarters.
- Always use both hands and hold him firmly (but not too tightly) against your body so he can't fall. Chihuahuas don't like to be held dangling in the air. Who would?
- Stay with your Chihuahua, especially if he's a puppy, when he's on the furniture. Left alone, he can jump off and hurt himself.

Don't

- Grab at your Chihuahua when you pick him up. This can frighten him.
- Stick your fingers between his rib cage and his front legs when you carry your dog. If you constantly hold your puppy this way, he'll walk with his elbows sticking out and his front legs won't be straight when he grows up.
- Squeeze the dog. This can hurt him and he might bite. Even the best-tempered dog will nip if he's hurt.

When he wakes up, take him outside to eliminate but don't fuss over him too much. Hopefully, he'll go back to sleep in his crate for the rest of the night when he's finished. As he becomes more comfortable in his new surroundings, he'll sleep through the night without whining or crying.

The First Veterinary Visit

Within the first 24 hours, and certainly not later than 72 hours from the time you pick him up, take your dog to your veterinarian for a complete physical.

Take along the information his breeder or rescue coordinator gave you about prior vaccines, so your veterinarian doesn't duplicate them.

Even if the breeder or rescue coordinator tells you that the dog is healthy or has already gone to a veterinarian, it's a good idea to take him to your own vet. You want to know that your Chi isn't suffering from a previously undiagnosed, chronic condition. If your dog is ill, your veterinarian can find it early and provide treatment.

Your Chihuahua should come with a health guarantee from the breeder or rescue organization. You can read more about the breeder's health guarantee in chapter 4. The first veterinary visit is a good time to ask the veterinarian any questions you have about your dog's care, behavior, and training.

Being a Responsible Owner

Having a dog means being completely responsible for him for the rest of his life. If you have a problem with your dog, find out how to solve it. The solution isn't to abandon your dog at a shelter. Thousands of dogs are put to death every year because their owners didn't care what happened to them. Don't add to this overwhelming pet problem.

Being a responsible owner also means respecting your neighbors' property and privacy. Your Chihuahua should never be allowed to defecate on a neighbor's lawn or wander around loose in the neighborhood. There's a strong chance he'll be poisoned, stolen, or hit by a car. Your dog could also pick up parasites, be bitten or attacked by another animal, or bite someone if he's frightened.

Some communities have ordinances requiring owners to clean up their dogs' messes left in public areas. Even if this is not the law in your area, always take a plastic bag with you to clean up after your dog and dispose of it in the proper waste container.

Don't let your dog bark incessantly outside, either, especially before eight o'clock in the morning or after ten o'clock at night. Barking dogs anger many people. Noisy dogs don't make good neighbors.

To pick up a Chihuahua, place one hand under his chest and the other behind his hindquarters.

Chapter 6

Feeding Your Chihuahua

Food, glorious dog food. There's definitely no shortage of bags and cans of canine cuisine. Walk into any pet supply store and you'll find a variety of recipes for dogs of all ages, sizes, and lifestyles. There are even special foods for dogs with medical problems. And if you don't have enough decisions to make already, food manufacturers also offer meals ranging from expensive premium foods with top ingredients to cheaper diets containing lesser-quality ingredients.

How do you know what's the healthiest choice for your Chihuahua's dining pleasure? Zero in on providing a well-balanced diet, avoid feeding too many treats, and maintain a regular feeding and exercise schedule. Good nutrition is the key to keeping little Miss Chi happy and healthy for a long time.

The best dog food for your Chihuahua should be well balanced and contain proteins, carbohydrates, fats, vitamins, and minerals for optimum nutrition. To see what ingredients are inside the bags or cans of commercial dog food, look on the labels. If they say "nutritionally complete" or "complete and balanced," they meet the minimum nutritional requirements for adults, puppies, and pregnant or lactating females, as established by the Association of American Feed Control Officials (AAFCO).

Choosing a Food

Once upon a time manufacturers made one kind of chow for all dogs to eat. Today there are so many recipes available that shoppers almost need a Dog Food 101 course just to know what their dogs should eat.

For Chihuahuas it's easy. They're toy dogs with tiny teeth, and they need a high-quality small-breed formula with ingredients you can recognize. The small-breed kibble recipes contain slightly more protein, fat, and calories than other formulas, and the kibble is a smaller size that's easier for little teeth to chew.

Have a Chi puppy? If so, buy the puppy recipe. Adults can eat a small-breed regular maintenance recipe, and senior Chis who are 10 or 11 years old will do fine on a senior recipe.

Stick to the premium brand, higher-priced foods that you don't usually see in supermarkets or large warehouse stores. You'll find them

Stick with a top-quality dog food that your dog loves and thrives on.

in smaller pet supply stores. Why pay more when there's cheaper dog food? The better foods use only top-quality ingredients that are easier for pets to digest. While the nutritional information on the labels of the premium and the bargain foods may look similar, they're really not. The type and percentages of proteins, carbohydrates, and fats in cheaper foods are really inferior ingredients.

Don't choose a food because it's advertised or a friend's Chihuahua does well on it. Not every dog thrives on the same food. And if you only have one Chihuahua, don't buy a gigantic bag, unless you plan to store it in an airtight container. While dry food doesn't go bad, it does get stale once it's opened. And let's face it, it's going to take a long time for a tiny Chi to go through a 60-pound bag of kibble!

Dry Kibble

To select a brand of commercial kibble, read the label to find out the ingredients. They are listed in order of quantity. Some substandard dog foods use animal by-products to maximize the amount of protein in the food. Much of this protein is useless because dogs can't digest it. Puppyhood is an especially crucial time for growth and development, and pups need quality ingredients to ensure that their bodies are receiving enough nutrients.

If your Chihuahua eats two meals a day, one meal should consist of dry food soaked in hot water for five minutes (be sure it has cooled before feeding). Mix the moistened food with a rounded tablespoon of canned food.

The second meal of the day should only be dry food. Kibble keeps the teeth clean. As your Chi chews her food, the dry pieces scrape against her teeth and remove any tartar that has accumulated.

Canned Food

With its meat-like consistency and tasty artificial flavoring, most dogs love canned food. The downside is that it's mostly water. This means you have to feed a lot more of it to achieve the same level of nutrition as you get in dry food. It has to be kept in the refrigerator once you open it, too.

Most Chi owners like to mix in about a tablespoon of canned food with the kibble.

Semi-moist Food

Here's a food with a chewy texture that's packaged in individual servings. Unfortunately, these portions are usually too much for a Chihuahua, so you'll have to wrap the leftovers up tightly and refrigerate them.

Semi-moist contains less water than canned, but it has a lot of salt, sugar, and food coloring, plus other preservatives, which isn't very healthy for your dog. Like canned, it's not good for your Chi's teeth, either. It sticks to the teeth and builds plaque, which leads to dental disease. This type of food is usually more expensive than dry food but costs less than canned.

Supplements

Besides all the dog food choices that are available, you'll also see various kinds of supplements for dogs. What are supplements, and should you give them to your Chihuahua? Veterinarians and breeders disagree about whether puppies need them or not. Many feel that if you feed your dog a good quality food, supplements aren't necessary. Others believe additional vitamins and minerals should be added if your Chi is a picky eater. There are many supplements on the market, but consult with your veterinarian before adding anything to your dog's diet.

Treats

For a treat once in a while, offer tiny dog biscuits. These come in small packages for small dogs and help keep teeth clean. One or two a day is probably okay, but don't substitute these biscuits for the dog's regular food. Too many snacks encourage finicky eating habits, and they don't have all the nutrients your dog needs for a balanced meal.

Reading Dog Food Labels

Dog food labels are not always easy to read, but if you know what to look for they can tell you a lot about what your dog is eating.

- The label should have a statement saying the dog food meets or exceeds the American Association of Feed Control Officials (AAFCO) nutritional guidelines. If the dog food doesn't meet AAFCO guidelines, it can't be considered complete and balanced, and can cause nutritional deficiencies.
- The guaranteed analysis lists the minimum percentages of crude protein and crude fat and the maximum percentages of crude fiber and water. AAFCO requires a minimum of 18 percent crude protein for adult dogs and 22 percent crude protein for puppies on a dry matter basis (that means with the water removed; canned foods should have more protein because they have more water). Dog food must also have a minimum of 5 percent crude fat for adults and 8 percent crude fat for puppies.
- The ingredients list the most common item in the food first, and so on, until you get to the least common item, which is listed last.
- Look for a dog food that lists an animal protein source first, such as chicken or poultry meal, beef or beef by-products, and that has other protein sources listed among the top five ingredients. That's because a food that lists chicken, wheat, wheat gluten, corn, and wheat fiber as the first five ingredients has more chicken than wheat, but may not have more chicken than all the grain products put together.
- Other ingredients may include a carbohydrate source, fat, vitamins and minerals, preservatives, fiber, and sometimes other additives purported to be healthy.
- Some grocery store brands may add artificial colors, sugar, and fillers—all of which should be avoided.

As with kibble, you'll see treats in all different sizes, shapes, ingredients, and flavors. Some cities even have gourmet bakeries with baked goods just for dogs! Although these treats are very cute and oh so tempting, they may contain preservatives, sugar, or artificial colorings and flavors that aren't healthy for your dog. Think of these as canine candy that needs to be given very sparingly.

If you want to feed your dog some people food, skip the fried foods, cooked bones, and fancy sauces and stick to giving her a few tiny pieces of chicken, turkey, cheese, fruits, steamed vegetables, cooked or hard-boiled eggs, cottage cheese, plain yogurt, peanut butter, plain pasta, or rice. These are healthy choices that your Chihuahua will happily gobble up, but put them into her dog bowl so she doesn't get into the habit of begging. If you mix them into her regular food, cut the fruits and veggies up into tiny pieces so that she won't be able to pick them out and leave the regular dog food.

Don't feed her from the table either! If you do that even once, she'll always beg for food while you're eating.

Homemade Diets

Feeding dogs homemade food has become a popular choice for some people who have concerns about commercial diets. Some recommend raw food and others use cooked meat. One advantage of these diets is that you have total control over what your dog is eating.

If you're contemplating preparing all of your Chihuahua's food yourself, do some homework first so that you can be sure to include all the vitamins and nutrients she needs. The homemade diet still needs to be well-balanced and a complete source of nutrition for your dog. This may be time-consuming, especially if you already have a busy schedule, because home-cooked recipes

A little treat now and then won't hurt. But make sure to subtract the day's treats when you are figuring out how much to feed your dog.

Tempted to include your Chihuahua in your dinner plans? Make sure you do your research and can prepare a complete and balanced diet for her.

include many ingredients that take time to properly prepare and store. Home cooking your Chi's food may also be more expensive than the commercial food.

You'll need to prepare your dog's food the same way you would your own food, with the proper refrigeration and storage, and serve it as fresh as possible. Raw meat, raw chicken, and uncooked eggs pose serious health risks. Traveling with your Chi when she's relying on a homemade diet may pose a challenge when you're on the road, too.

When and How Much?

Before bringing your new Chihuahua home, ask the breeder or rescue coordinator what kind and how much food your Chi was eating. Find out how many times a day she was fed and if there were designated meal times. Keep everything the same for at least the first few days before gradually changing to a schedule that fits in with your lifestyle.

A puppy should eat four meals a day until you see that she's leaving food in the dish. At this point, it's time to cut down to three meals, spread out throughout the day and evening. Don't cut the total daily amount of food down, just the number of meals. That means you will feed your dog a little more at each meal. In fact, if your Chi seems hungrier at each meal, add an extra tablespoon of food.

> ## Changing Your Dog's Diet
>
> When you pick your dog up, you may receive a small quantity of the same food your Chihuahua has been eating. Use this, or your own supply of the same food, for your Chi's first few meals.
>
> If you want to change your new Chihuahua's diet, don't do it right away. Give her at least a week or two to feel settled into her new digs. After that, it's okay to switch foods, but do it gradually over several days. If you change the menu too quickly, it will upset your Chi's stomach and she's liable to have diarrhea.
>
> When you're ready, mix in some of the new food with the old food—about one-quarter of the new stuff. Add a little more of the new food each day, until it has entirely replaced the previous diet. Remember, the total amount of food you're feeding at each meal remains the same.

Your puppy will let you know when it's time to cut down to two meals a day, spaced about ten to twelve hours apart. Again, she will begin to leave food in the bowl on the three-meals-per-day schedule. Increase the portions given at each meal when you switch to two meals a day.

If your Chi shows signs of still being hungry—she wolfs her meal down quickly, licks the bowl, and gives you a look that says "More please"—give her a little more. Each puppy is an individual, and just as people eat different size portions, so do Chihuahuas.

Adult Chihuahuas should eat two meals a day. It takes a little trial and error to determine how much food you should offer at each meal, but stick to the schedule and feed her at about the same time every day.

Establish a Feeding Schedule

Dogs like routines. They have very accurate inner alarm clocks, and if you're running late or forget to feed them, they'll loudly alert you when it's time to eat. Establishing set feeding times and sticking to them (within an hour or so) lets your Chihuahua know what to expect. Feeding puppies at fixed times will help with housetraining, too. When your pup finishes her meal, you'll know she needs to be taken outside to eliminate.

Running on Empty

Puppies younger than 4 months of age are particularly susceptible to developing hypoglycemia, which means their blood sugar level has dipped too low. Potentially life-threatening to Chihuahuas and other small dogs, hypoglycemia can occur at any age, especially when dogs have had too much exercise, they're stressed, or they haven't eaten in a while.

The symptoms of hypoglycemia include trembling, lethargy, seeming to be dazed or confused, or acting uncoordinated. If left untreated, hypoglycemia can cause seizures, collapse, or loss of consciousness, and can even be fatal.

Keep a little corn syrup or honey in the house at all times, and if you notice your Chi showing any signs of this problem, rub a little corn syrup or honey in her mouth. Give her a few minutes to perk up and give her another dose. Immediately feed her a regular meal and then take her to the veterinarian.

If you have a puppy who is prone to being hypoglycemic, feed her a high-quality food four to five times a day. Between meals you can also give her a few healthy, high-calorie snacks.

Too Many Calories, Not Enough Exercise

It's tough to overfeed a puppy, but if your adult dog has become a couch potato, it's probably wise to cut back the amount of fat and calories she is consuming. If your Chihuahua is weighing in at twelve pounds and is only seven inches tall, she's obese! Carrying excess weight puts too much pressure on the dog's heart and legs and makes it difficult for her to move around or breathe properly.

When a Chihuahua is at a normal weight, you should be able to feel but not see her ribs. Her body should also have a definite shape to it—and that doesn't mean being perfectly round!

While there are "light" dog food formulas developed especially for over-weight dogs, consider giving your overweight Chihuahua some additional exercise and cutting down on the amount of regular food you're feeding her. This is a healthier way to take off a few ounces.

The Picky Eater

While some Chihuahuas will always pick at their food, there are a few things you can do to encourage good eating habits. Give your adult Chihuahua only ten minutes to eat her meal. If she hasn't finished in that time, pick up the food

Forbidden Foods

Dogs love chocolate, but under *no* circumstances should your Chihuahua eat even one small bite of it. Dogs are unable to digest chocolate, and bigger amounts can be fatal.

There are other foods that are also hazardous to your dog's health and may cause an upset stomach, vomiting, diarrhea, or an allergic reaction. These include onions, seeds, grapes, raisins, macadamia nuts, all alcoholic beverages, and spicy, greasy, or salty foods.

Never give your dog any cooked chicken, turkey, pork, or beef bones. The ends can splinter and slice your dog's intestines, or she can choke.

dish and throw the food away. This teaches her that she'd better eat it when it's given to her, or else it's gone. Don't even feel sorry for your Chi. A healthy dog will eat before she starves. And a dog who lingers over food for half an hour or more is likely to become a picky eater.

Leaving the bowl down all day doesn't solve the problem, either. She'll just wander away, knowing it will still be there if she decides to come back. Besides, if the food is always there you won't be able to tell when she's sick and really doesn't feel like eating.

The exception is if you have a Chihuahua who is hypoglycemic; in that case, you'll need to leave a small amount of dry food out all the time. Make sure she does eat something every few hours, even if it means enticing her with a little peanut butter or yogurt.

Hopefully, you're not giving her table scraps or too many treats throughout the day, either. Most dogs would rather eat treats than their regular meals (can you blame them?), so cut out the goodies!

Little dogs need small portions of food. Overweight dogs are prone to a wide variety of health problems.

No matter where you go with your dog, always bring your own water from home or give her bottled water.

Switching to another food may work in the beginning with a picky eater, but after a while she'll become bored with that one, too. Don't get started on that cycle with your dog. You can also try warming up her food and staying around while she eats. If you set the food down and walk away, some Chihuahuas would rather follow you than eat.

Occasionally, a dog won't want to eat anything for a day or two. If she seems okay otherwise, she's probably all right. But if her appetite hasn't returned by the middle of the second day, contact your veterinarian because your Chi may be ill.

Clean Water

Fresh, clean water must be available for your Chihuahua at all times. Be sure to thoroughly wash the bowl and refill it with fresh water every day. Dogs who eat mostly dry kibble will drink more water.

If you take your Chi traveling with you, don't let her drink from other water sources, such as a trough at a dog park or from a motel faucet. Always bring a water supply from home or use bottled water. Different cities have different chemicals in their water, and unfamiliar water may upset your Chi's delicate tummy.

Don't use any disinfectant to wash your Chihuahua's dishes, because the dog will smell the disinfectant even if you don't. The dog may refuse to drink or eat from the bowls, becoming dangerously dehydrated.

Chapter 7

Grooming Your Chihuahua

What will the well-dressed Chihuahua be wearing this year? No doubt the latest designer doggy duds, fresh off the canine runways. Today, clothing made especially for Chihuahuas and other toy dogs is all the rage with bow wow boutiques all over the Internet and in just about every retail store.

Want your Chi to look like he's ready to hop on a Harley in a leather vest and cap? Do combat fatigues and army booties suit your macho Chi? Or is your Chi more the outdoor type, preferring a basic flannel jacket and matching hat with earflaps? You can find virtually any type of four-legged outfit imaginable, and if you can't find what you're looking for, it can probably be custom-made to fit your tiny one.

Then again, if you'd rather not have a clotheshorse for a Chihuahua, you can always accessorize with a hot new designer leash and flashy matching collar. You'll find everything from floral to jeweled to holiday motifs to suit your and your dog's every whim.

Sure you want your dog to look his best, but beautiful designer fashions only go skin deep. Beneath that white pirate shirt, red sash, and swashbuckler chapeau is a Chihuahua who needs to be groomed. Perhaps you selected this breed because you didn't want to fuss with a foo-foo dog who needs fancy haircuts or hours of brushing. But a Chihuahua does have a few little things that must be done to keep him in good physical condition.

No matter what the fashion preference of you and your Chihuahua, you can find the clothes that make the dog.

Why Groom a Smooth?

Whether your Chi is longhaired or short, he needs his teeth and coat brushed every day, his toenails clipped once a week, and a dip in the bathtub sometime during the month. Eyes and ears should be checked daily, too. If you've never cared for a dog before, the first few grooming sessions may be a little stressful until you get the hang of it, but you'll be an old hand in no time.

Because the Long Coat Chihuahua takes minutes to brush and the Smooth practically no time at all, grooming a Chihuahua is easy. Your Chi will enjoy it, too, and you can tell that he just feels better when he's clean and mat-free. Another bonus to your dog's spa treatment is that he'll be more accustomed to handling, so that when it comes time to visit the veterinarian he'll be more comfortable when someone else touches him all over.

No one likes to find dog hair all over the furniture or carpet, which is why daily brushing is recommended. It keeps dog hair on the grooming brush and not dispersed throughout every room of the house. Whether your Chihuahua is a Long Coat or a Smooth, prepare to brush (and vacuum)! You would think hair from a Long Coat is more work to clean up, but it's actually much easier. Long Coat hair scoops up in a clump, but loose Smooth hairs are spikey and stick into everything!

Yes, even the Smooth Coat needs regular grooming.

Begin the beauty treatments when your dog is a puppy. Keep your sessions short and sweet so he'll learn to like them. Give him a small food treat when you're finished bathing, brushing, or trimming toenails. To make the process easier, set aside at least one day a week when you won't be rushed and can take the time you need for your Chi. Think of the grooming session as a relaxing, bonding experience with your dog.

Grooming Supplies

There are several items you'll need:

- Hard rubber comb (not nylon or plastic)
- Flea comb
- Natural bristle brush
- Baby or dog shampoo
- Medicated shampoo (if there are skin problems)
- Cotton balls
- Strips of rolled cotton
- Nail clippers or cordless, battery-operated nail grinder
- Styptic powder or pencil (a coagulating agent)
- Slicker brush (for the Long Coats)
- Mat splitter (for the Long Coats)
- Canine toothbrush and toothpaste
- Blow dryer
- Cotton bath towels

If you can afford to buy a grooming table with a nonskid surface and a grooming noose that holds your dog's head still, it's well worth the expense. You'll be able to brush your Chi and clip his toenails without having to bend over. You can also use an outdoor picnic table, a kitchen or bathroom counter, or any raised surface. Place a rubber mat on the top so your dog's feet won't slide.

Before you begin grooming your dog, assemble all the materials you'll be using. This way, you won't have to stop in the middle to get something.

Getting Started

Come grooming day, start by checking over your dog's skin. Look for signs of external parasites, such as fleas or ticks. (There's more about these nasty little bugs later in this chapter.) Use a flea comb to help you detect any fleas that may be hiding beneath your Chi's tail, on his hips, or even near his head. If you don't see any of the little pests, look for flea dirt, which looks like tiny bits of pepper. If you find any, it means your dog does have fleas but they've gone undercover by burrowing deep into your Chi's coat. Your veterinarian has flea preventives that will get rid of them (see the box on page 83).

Be sure to look for any ticks between your dog's toes, in his ears, or around his neck and rear. If you find one of these parasites, remove it immediately, as described in the box on page 72.

Next, check your dog for any skin abrasions, bruises, red areas, and other abnormalities such as lumps or skin infections. When you spot a problem early on, you can take care of it before it gets worse.

Run your hands over your Chihuahua's entire body. This stimulates the skin and gives you an opportunity to find anything abnormal. Your Chi won't object to this examination; in fact, most dogs like it.

When your dog is on the grooming table (or any elevated surface), *keep one hand on him at all times*. Don't leave him up there if you have to walk away, even for a minute. It won't take much for your Chi to wiggle around, fall off, and injure himself.

Brushing Your Chi

Believe it or not, Chihuahuas do shed. If you want to cut down on the amount of loose dog hair floating around your house, brush your Chi every day, or at least three times a week. Your Chihuahua will be cleaner and need fewer baths. Besides, it only takes a few minutes.

A Chihuahua's coat grows in cycles. It will grow for a while, stop, dry out, then shed. It usually takes about 125 to 135 days to complete

> **TIP**
>
> Use natural bristle and hard rubber brushes because nylon brushes and combs can cause static electricity, particularly if the air in your house is very dry during the winter.

How to Get Rid of a Tick

Although Frontline, K-9 Advantix, and BioSpot, the new generation of flea fighters, are partially effective in killing ticks once they are on your dog, they are not 100 percent effective and will not keep ticks from biting your dog in the first place. During tick season (which, depending on where you live, can be spring, summer, and/or fall), examine your dog every day for ticks. Pay particular attention to your dog's neck, behind the ears, the armpits, and the groin.

When you find a tick, use a pair of tweezers to grasp the tick as close as possible to the dog's skin and pull it out using firm, steady pressure. Check to make sure you get the whole tick (mouth parts left in your dog's skin can cause an infection), then dab the wound with a little hydrogen peroxide and some antibiotic ointment. Watch for signs of inflammation.

Ticks carry very serious diseases that are transmittable to humans, so dispose of the tick safely. *Never* crush it between your fingers. Don't flush it down the toilet either, because the tick will survive the trip and infect another animal. Instead, use the tweezers to place the tick in a tight-sealing jar or plastic dish with a little alcohol, put on the lid, and dispose of the container in an outdoor garbage can. Wash the tweezers thoroughly with hot water and alcohol.

the cycle, but this time frame varies. Most dogs shed their winter coats in the spring, but not Chihuahuas. Since they're in a warm house all the time, they don't need to build up a heavy coat to protect them from the cold outdoors. Lucky you! Instead of having a predictable shedding time, Chis shed all year long.

Daily brushing not only keeps your house clean, but also gets out the dead coat that is shedding and stimulates new hair growth. And on Long Coats, it keeps tangles and mats from forming.

Use a natural bristle brush on the body coat and a hard rubber comb on the ear fringe, legs, and leg fringes. The tail plume will take a brush and a hard rubber comb.

With the dog on your lap, right side up, or on a nonslip table with the head away from you and the rear end of the puppy toward your body, start at the base of the spine and begin brushing by stroking in the opposite direction to the way the coat is growing. Going in the opposite direction for a few strokes gets the dead hair out quickly. Finish the routine by brushing in the direction the coat is growing, from the back of the neck down the spine, along the body sides and toward the tail.

Also be sure to brush your Chi's tummy. While he's still on your lap, lay your Chi on his back and brush his neck, chest, and belly. Return the dog to his right side up position on your lap. Now comb the fine hairs of the ear fringe, the leg furnishings, and the legs with the hard rubber comb. The tail plume may be brushed first, then finished with the hard rubber comb. The entire brushing and combing should take about five minutes.

The longhaired Chi will tangle behind his elbows and ears, and along the tail. To untangle mats, which are clumps of fine hair stuck together, use a soft slicker brush or a detangling spray. You may also separate the hairs with a special grooming tool called a mat splitter or separate each hair, little by little, until the mat is removed. If mats are a persistent problem, particularly the very fine hairs of the ear fringe, you may have to brush your dog several times a week, or else your Chi needs a bath.

On a Long Coat, it may be necessary to trim just a little of the hair around the anus so the area can be kept clean during bowel movements. Do not trim unless the rear end constantly gets dirty.

When the job is done, wipe your dog down with a damp towel or give him a light spray of mink oil, which is available at most pet supply stores. This gives his coat a nice shine and keeps all his hair in place.

A metal flea comb is useful for grooming sensitive areas, such as around the face.

Trimming Nails

Trimming your dog's nails nice and short isn't just a beauty treatment; it's a health issue. When his nails are too long, it forces your Chi to walk on the balls of his feet, which may throw him off balance. It doesn't take much for your delicate little dog to fall and possibly break a leg, especially if he walks or runs on a slippery surface. Long nails are more apt to tear and cause pain, too.

Some people think walking on concrete automatically keeps a dog's nails short, but this isn't true. Some dogs just naturally have toenails that grow faster or slower than other dogs', no matter what surface they spend a lot of time on.

How short should your Chihuahua's nails be? If you can hear them clicking on the floor when he walks, they're too long. When they begin curling over the tops of the feet, it's time for a trim. Left undone, they will continue to curl and can actually grow into the bottom of your dog's feet. Ouch!

For the healthiest feet, trim your Chihuahua's nails once a week. At the same time, trim the hair between your Chi's foot pads, which gives them that dainty look Chihuahuas are known for. The longer you wait between pedicures, the longer the nails grow and the more time it takes to cut them. Choose the same day of the week for nail trimming. This just makes it easier to remember.

Trimming your dog's nails is important for his health. Even city dogs who walk on concrete pavement need an occasional trim.

Choose a day that you know you won't be rushed or interrupted and can take your time. When the time comes, assemble all the tools you'll need before you pick up your dog.

To prepare your dog for his first clipping experience, spend a week or two turning the nail grinder on and off several times so your Chi becomes accustomed to the noise. Handle his feet and gently rub his toes repeatedly in short sessions of no longer than five or six minutes. With your forefinger and thumb, apply gentle pressure on each toe so that your dog becomes accustomed to his toes being spread apart. While some dogs are fine with their feet being handled, others need more time to learn to relax.

When your Chihuahua seems comfortable with toe touching, have some tasty treats on hand to use as positive reinforcement after each nail is trimmed. These will help him associate the experience with receiving a reward. To clip nails, put your Chi up on the grooming table and spend a few minutes petting him and talking to him so he relaxes. Some people prefer to sit on the couch with their Chi lying next to them. Try out both positions to see what works out the best for you and your dog.

Begin by picking up one paw and holding it firmly but gently on the pad of the foot, between your finger and thumb. Using the nail clippers or the grinder, cut off the white part or just the hook-like tip of your dog's toenail slightly above the quick—the blood vessel that looks like a dark cone in the middle of the nail.

If you cut off too much, the nail may bleed, so be prepared to use a styptic powder or pencil to stop the bleeding. You can also apply cornstarch if you don't have styptic powder. Dip your finger into the styptic powder and press against the nail for a moment until the powder or pencil absorbs the blood. Don't worry. Even professional groomers accidentally clip a little too much sometimes. Your dog will not bleed to death.

After the first nail, give your dog a treat—a small piece of apple, cheese, or hot dog, or a lick of peanut butter works wonders. If he is too stressed, end the session but resume the job later on or the next day.

Don't quit! The more you trim your dog's nails, the more confidence you'll have. Continue trimming as many nails as both of you can handle in a session, being sure to let your dog relax a little between toes. In no time at all, your Chihuahua will be eager for a pedicure.

Bathing Your Chihuahua

Keeping your Chi's skin and coat healthy and in good condition doesn't begin with a bath. It starts from the inside with a healthy diet. When you feed your dog a diet that's rich in the essential vitamins and minerals (see chapter 6) you'll see the results in a lustrous, glossy coat that no pet shampoo can duplicate.

Whether he's a Smooth or a Long Coat, your Chihuahua doesn't need a bath more often than once a month, unless he's dirty or has a doggy smell you don't care for. It's amazing how regular brushing removes a lot of the dust and grime in a coat, but it won't rid your dog of the natural oil build-up that gives every dog that special *eau de canine* fragrance. Here's where a monthly bath restores your Chi to his former sweet-smelling self.

But don't plunk your dog in the bathtub. Chihuahuas are tiny enough for bathing in your kitchen sink, and this is a great place to do the job. It's waist high, so you won't have to bend way over like you would if you used the bathtub. Be sure to put a small rubber bathmat on the bottom of the sink so your dog won't slip and slide. You can even use a dish mat! If your sink has a hose attachment, you're good to go; if not, you can always rinse the shampoo off with a plastic pitcher. Use the sink stopper but don't clamp it down all the way. Leave it slightly loose so some water can stay in the sink and some can drain away.

Check that there isn't a draft coming from a vent or an open window. You don't want your Chi to catch a chill! Then begin the bath by testing the water to make sure it's not too hot or too cold. To keep water from getting into your Chihuahua's ears, place some cotton in each ear (not too far down), but don't forget to remove it when the bath is over.

Wet your dog thoroughly and massage a small amount of either mild baby shampoo or canine shampoo throughout his coat. If your dog has skin problems, there are gentle, medicated shampoos for various skin and coat conditions that your veterinarian can recommend.

Don't forget to wash your Chi's tummy, tail plume, and all the fringes of the ears and legs. Put a tiny amount of shampoo on your fingertips or onto a washcloth and carefully soap up your Chi's head. Be careful not to get any soap in his eyes. If you do, rinse it out promptly with clean water. When you're finished shampooing, rinse your dog thoroughly. If there's any soap residue left on the coat, your dog will itch and his coat will be dull and flaky.

If you're using a coat conditioner, apply it after you've rinsed your dog, and be sure to rinse out the conditioner.

Drying Your Chihuahua

To dry the coat, use thick, all-cotton towels for good water absorption or a canine hair dryer. Using a dryer is quicker and keeps your dog from getting a chill while he's drying out. Tiny Chis get cold easily. Just make sure that the dryer temperature isn't too hot so you don't burn your baby!

If you have a Long Coat, blow dry in the direction the coat grows—from the neck toward the tail. When the coat is thoroughly dry, run a finishing glove over the coat to give it an extra sheen. Pat your dog dry to remove any excess

A Long Coat will likely need more frequent bathing. Don't forget to wash the tail plume and all the fringes.

moisture. Use another towel to gently massage your dog. This will stimulate the skin.

Use a hard rubber comb to comb out the ears, the leg fringes, and the tail plume.

Ear Care

Check your dog's ears every day to make sure they are clean and healthy. When ears are healthy, they are pink on the inside and the edges are free of splits or tears. There should be no odor. If you see a black substance in the ear or smell a foul odor, this may just be a waxy buildup that needs to be cleaned out or a sign of ear mites.

If your Chihuahua constantly shakes his head, continually scratches his ears, frequently tilts his head to one side, or rubs his head on the floor, he may have an ear infection. Your veterinarian should examine your Chi's ears.

Healthy ears are pink on the inside and have no odor.

Dental Hygiene

All breeds need regular oral care for both gums and teeth. According to the American Veterinary Dental Society (AVDS), 80 percent of dogs develop gum disease by 3 years of age. This organization believes that with regular veterinary dental checkups and proper home care, canine gum disease can be eliminated. Symptoms of gum disease are tartar around the gum line, swollen and red gums, bleeding gums, loose teeth, oral abscesses, and bad breath. Prevention is the first step. Have your veterinarian check for evidence of plaque; it can be kept under control by brushing your dog's teeth several times per week.

Keeping teeth clean need not be a chore if you introduce the proper techniques while your Chihuahua is young. Get the puppy accustomed to having his teeth brushed every day. Brushing with plain warm water is better than not doing it at all, but using a canine toothpaste is better yet. It dissolves without rinsing and dogs love the taste! Don't use a toothpaste made for humans; it will give your dog an upset stomach.

Start brushing your Chi's teeth every day in puppyhood, and continue the oral care for his entire life. If you don't, tartar builds up and bacteria in the mouth can enter the bloodstream. Once the bacteria are in the bloodstream, they travel to the heart and other organs and cause infection and heart problems.

Use the smallest size canine toothbrush and doggy toothpaste. Don't worry about rinsing out your Chihuahua's mouth after brushing. Canine toothpaste dissolves in the mouth and is made especially for dogs. Once your Chi becomes accustomed to the procedure, he'll look forward to it because he'll like the taste.

To begin, open your Chi's mouth and rub your fingers or a soft gauze pad gently over his gums. After a few days, when he tolerates this routine, begin to use a soft canine tooth-brush. Start by just touching the toothbrush to the teeth, then apply a little pressure. In a day or two, move the brush around the front of the

It will be easier to keep your dog's teeth clean if you get him used to having his mouth touched early on.

teeth, gradually moving to the rear molars. Although it will not be your puppy's favorite part of the grooming routine, he'll learn to tolerate the brushing.

Keep up with the brushing, and once every six months take your Chihuahua to the veterinarian for a more thorough cleaning. Chew toys help keep your Chihuahua's teeth clean, too.

Eye Care

Chihuahuas' eyes require little care, other than stray hair getting into their eyes or tear staining. You can easily trim long strands of hair that bother your dog, but getting rid of tear stains is a little more difficult. Staining can be caused by small tear ducts or eyes that naturally protrude. To keep bacteria or dirt from accumulating around the tear ducts, clean the eyes every day by wiping them with distilled water.

More serious causes of tear staining include entropion, a condition caused by the eyelashes rubbing against the eye. As the eyelashes constantly rub against the cornea, an ulcer may result. Ectropion is another name for a sagging lower eye-lid. This will allow all sorts of dirt to enter the eye surface and may cause con-junctivitis. Fortunately, these two problems are not common to the Chihuahua.

As soon as you notice tear staining on your puppy's face, ask your veterinar-ian to examine your Chihuahua's eyes. There are veterinary ophthalmologists

Making Your Environment Flea Free

If there are fleas on your dog, there are fleas in your home, yard, and car, even if you can't see them. Take these steps to combat them.

In your home:

- Wash whatever is washable (the dog bed, sheets, blankets, pillow covers, slipcovers, curtains, etc.).
- Vacuum everything else in your home—furniture, floors, rugs, everything. Pay special attention to the folds and crevices in upholstery, cracks between floorboards, and the spaces between the floor and the baseboards. Flea larvae are sensitive to sunlight, so inside the house they prefer deep carpet, bedding, and cracks and crevices.
- When you're done, throw the vacuum cleaner bag away—in an outside garbage can.
- Use a nontoxic flea-killing powder, such as Flea Busters or Zodiac FleaTrol, to treat your carpets (but remember, it does not control fleas elsewhere in the house). The powder stays deep in the carpet and kills fleas (using a form of boric acid) for up to a year.
- If you have a particularly serious flea problem, consider using a fogger or long-lasting spray to kill any adult and larval fleas, or having a professional exterminator treat your home.

who specialize in eye problems and your veterinarian may recommend one if the tear staining can't be cured with common methods or medications. Daily eye care is a must for a dog who has constant tear staining.

External Parasites

Today there are new ways to prevent fleas and ticks from bothering your dog. Some flea and tick prevention and management programs are available only through your veterinarian, while others are over-the-counter products. These flea and tick management programs can usually get rid of, or at least control, this problem, by breaking the infestation cycle of the parasite. The suggestions in the box above for making an environment flea free will also help control ticks and mites.

In your car:

- Take out the floor mats and hose them down with a strong stream of water, then hang them up to dry in the sun.
- Wash any towels, blankets, or other bedding you regularly keep in the car.
- Thoroughly vacuum the entire interior of your car, paying special attention to the seams between the bottom and back of the seats.
- When you're done, throw the vacuum cleaner bag away—in an outside garbage can.

In your yard:

- Flea larvae prefer shaded areas that have plenty of organic material and moisture, so rake the yard thoroughly and bag all the debris in tightly sealed bags.
- Spray your yard with an insecticide that has residual activity for at least thirty days. Insecticides that use a form of boric acid are nontoxic. Some newer products contain an insect growth regulator (such as fenoxycarb) and need to be applied only once or twice a year.
- For an especially difficult flea problem, consider having an exterminator treat your yard.
- Keep your yard free of piles of leaves, weeds, and other organic debris. Be especially careful in shady, moist areas, such as under bushes.

Fleas

Flea bites are irritating and can cause itchy red skin on both humans and dogs. They may also cause an allergic reaction or transmit tapeworm to dogs. To keep fleas under control, they must be eliminated from your dog and the home environment, inside and out, as well as from your car if your dog travels with you. Many flea sprays and flea bombs are available for this purpose. See the box above.

Ticks

Ticks carry Lyme disease and other ailments, such as Rocky Mountain spotted fever, which can affect dog and human alike. The deer tick that carries Lyme disease is extremely tiny and may not be readily visible to the naked eye.

Fleas can torment your dog with their itchy bites.

If you see a tick on your dog, do not touch it with your fingers because if it is carrying a disease, you could become infected. After pulling out the tick (as described in the box on page 72), you may notice that the head is still embedded under the skin. Dab it with a little antibiotic ointment and it should fall off in a few days.

Mange

Hair loss, skin inflammation, or lesions are signs of mange, which is caused by a microscopic mite. Depending on the type of mange, the hair loss will either start at the head and ears or somewhere on the body, and it can easily spread. Mange can be a very serious condition if it is not treated promptly. There are all kinds of shampoos, ointments, dips, and drugs available today to control the mange mite. Although mange is not a common problem, it is more apt to show up in puppies than in adult dogs.

New Products in the Fight Against Fleas

At one time, battling fleas meant exposing your dog and yourself to toxic dips, sprays, powders, and collars. But today there are flea preventives that work very well and are safe for your dog, you, and the environment. The two most common types are insect growth regulators (IGRs), which stop the immature flea from developing or maturing, and adult flea killers. To deal with an active infestation, experts usually recommend a product that has both.

These next-generation flea fighters generally come in one of two forms:

- **Topical treatments or spot-on.** These products are applied to the skin, usually between the shoulder blades. The product is absorbed through the skin into the dog's system. Among the most widely available spot-on are Advantage (kills adult fleas and larvae), Revolution (kills adult fleas), Frontline Plus (kills adult fleas and larvae, plus an IGR), K-9 Advantix (kills adult fleas and larvae), and BioSpot (kills adult fleas and larvae, plus an IGR).
- **Systemic products.** This is a pill your dog swallows that transmits a chemical throughout the dog's bloodstream. When a flea bites the dog, it picks up this chemical, which then prevents the flea's eggs from developing. Among the most widely available systemic products are Program (kills larvae only, plus an IGR) and Capstar (kills adult fleas).

Make sure you read all the labels and apply the products exactly as recommended, and that you check to make sure they are safe for puppies.

Chapter 8

Keeping Your Chihuahua Healthy

A Chi may act like a bigshot on the outside, but when she's feeling under the weather, there's a tiny, delicate dog on the inside who needs your help. Chihuahuas weigh an average of less than six pounds and can't afford to lose any weight if they're ill.

To keep your Chi in good shape, provide good veterinary and preventive care, plus a healthy lifestyle. With an average life span of 12 to 17 years, the Chihuahua is sturdier than she appears, but your Chi's road to wellness begins with a good foundation. A complete series of vaccinations; flea, tick, and heartworm preventives; and spaying or neutering your dog will prevent some of the most dangerous canine conditions. Don't forget her regular grooming, good dental care, nutritious diet, and proper exercise. These give her the best assurance of a long and active life.

Choosing a Veterinarian

When it comes to safeguarding your Chi's health, your veterinarian is the professional you can rely on. If you don't already have a veterinarian, choosing one should be at the top of your priority list. Don't wait until your pet is sick to look for a vet, because you won't have time to interview candidates. Plan to find a doctor before your dog comes home, or at least within the first two days.

To find the names of veterinarians, contact the American Animal Hospital Association (see the appendix) or ask your dog's breeder, rescue coordinator, and other Chihuahua and small dog owners for referrals. Finding a veterinarian who's fairly close to you is convenient.

What should you look for in a veterinarian? While you might think your Chi's veterinarian should specialize in small dog medicine, most veterinarians don't limit their practices to dogs of a certain size. A good veterinarian, though, is knowledgeable about all breeds and keeps up with the latest health developments.

When interviewing veterinarians, ask about health conditions Chihuahuas are more likely to have (they're listed later in this chapter) and how the veterinarian would treat them. The explanations should be fairly easy to understand. This will give you an idea of what it will be like to communicate with that vet if your Chi has a problem later

Look for a veterinarian who handles your dog in a way that makes both of you feel comfortable.

on. Don't go to any veterinarian you don't feel comfortable with or who won't take the time to explain things to you. The veterinarian should also like small dogs and be happy to see your Chi whenever she visits.

Another question to ask when interviewing veterinarians is how many doctors are on staff. Having more than one veterinarian in the office means that someone is always available to see your dog during the daytime. Some veterinarians provide after-hours care, but most refer patients to an emergency clinic they confer with.

Since your Chi will be interacting with the technicians too, ask what qualifications they must have before they are hired. You're looking for an experienced, knowledgeable team to help treat your dog. Ask for a tour of the hospital facilities to see if they are clean and orderly. A good veterinary office should be very willing to schedule an appointment to show you around. Be prepared to pay for their time.

Holistic Medicine

While many veterinarians treat patients with conventional forms of medicine that have been tested using scientific experimentation and clinical trials, others may recommend holistic medicine, which incorporates alternative treatments such as acupuncture, chiropractic care, and botanical and homeopathic remedies.

Vaccines

What vaccines dogs need and how often they need them has been a subject of controversy for several years. Researchers, health care professionals, vaccine manufacturers, and dog owners do not always agree on which vaccines each dog needs or how often booster shots must be given.

In 2006, the American Animal Hospital Association issued a set of vaccination guidelines and recommendations intended to help dog owners and veterinarians sort through much of the controversy and conflicting information. The guidelines designate four vaccines as core, or essential for every dog, because of the serious nature of the diseases and their widespread distribution. These are canine distemper virus (using a modified live virus or recombinant modified live virus vaccine), canine parvovirus (using a modified live virus vaccine), canine adenovirus-2 (using a modified live virus vaccine), and rabies (using a killed virus). The general recommendations for their administration (except rabies, for which you must follow local laws) are:

- Vaccinate puppies at 6–8 weeks, 9–11 weeks, and 12–14 weeks.
- Give an initial "adult" vaccination when the dog is older than 16 weeks; two doses, three to four weeks apart,

According to the American Holistic Veterinary Association (AHVA), the techniques used in holistic medicine are gentle and minimally invasive, and they incorporate patient well-being and stress reduction. Holistic medicine, as practiced by a qualified veterinarian, can provide you with many options for treating your Chihuahua. While some alternative therapies are better than others, it's tempting to try anything if your dog doesn't respond to conventional techniques.

Some veterinarians specialize in holistic medicine while others combine conventional and alternative methods. To find holistic veterinarians in your area, contact the AHVA (see the appendix).

are advised, but one dose is considered protective and acceptable.

- Give a booster shot when the dog is 1 year old.
- Give a subsequent booster shot every three years, unless there are risk factors that make it necessary to vaccinate more or less often.

Noncore vaccines should only be considered for those dogs who risk exposure to a particular disease because of geographic area, lifestyle, frequency of travel, or other issues. They include vaccines against distemper-measles virus, canine parainfluenza virus, leptospirosis, Bordetella bronchiseptica, and Borrelia burgdorferi (Lyme disease).

Vaccines that are not generally recommended because the disease poses little risk to dogs or is easily treatable, or the vaccine has not been proven to be effective, are those against Giardia, canine coronavirus, and canine adenovirus-1.

Often, combination injections are given to puppies, with one shot containing several core and noncore vaccines. Your veterinarian may be reluctant to use separate shots that do not include the noncore vaccines, because they must be specially ordered. If you are concerned about these noncore vaccines, talk to your vet.

The First Veterinary Visit

When it's time for your Chi's first visit to the veterinarian, bring along a fresh stool sample. The veterinarian should examine it to see if your dog has internal parasites, such as roundworms, whipworms, tapeworms, and hookworms.

This is a great time to ask your veterinarian about setting up a preventive health plan for your Chihuahua. Once you know what to expect, you'll be able to plan for your dog's regular care. If you have any questions about your little one's behavior or nutrition, be sure to ask the doctor. Your Chihuahua will also need preventative flea, tick, and heartworm medication and spaying or neutering.

Regular checkups will keep your dog healthy and help her live a long life.

Preventive Care

One way to monitor your Chi's health is to take her to the veterinarian once a year for a routine checkup. During the annual visit she'll receive any vaccinations she might need. This is also a good time for your veterinarian to detect any problems that may not be obvious to you, such as heart, kidney, liver, or dental disease; cancer; or parasites.

Why Spay and Neuter?

Breeding dogs is a serious undertaking that should only be part of a well-planned breeding program. Why? Because dogs pass on their physical and behavioral problems to their offspring. Even healthy, well-behaved dogs can pass on problems in their genes.

Is your dog so sweet that you'd like to have a litter of puppies just like her? If you breed her to another dog, the pups will not have the same genetic heritage she has. Breeding her *parents* again will increase the odds of a similar pup, but even then, the puppies in the second litter could inherit different genes. In fact, *there is no way to breed a dog to be just like another dog.*

Meanwhile, thousands and thousands of dogs are killed in animal shelters every year simply because they have no homes. Casual breeding is a big contributor to this problem.

If you don't plan to breed your dog, is it still a good idea to spay her or neuter him? Yes!

When you spay your female:

- You avoid her heat cycles, during which she discharges blood and scent.
- It greatly reduces the risk of mammary cancer and eliminates the risk of pyometra (an often fatal infection of the uterus) and uterine cancer.
- It prevents unwanted pregnancies.
- It reduces dominance behaviors and aggression.

When you neuter your male:

- It curbs the desire to roam and to fight with other males.
- It greatly reduces the risk of prostate cancer and eliminates the risk of testicular cancer.
- It helps reduce leg lifting and mounting behavior.
- It reduces dominance behaviors and aggression.

Chihuahua puppies are delicate little animals, and breeding them is best left to the experts.

Chihuahua Health Issues

All purebred and mixed-breed dogs, including Chihuahuas, inherit diseases and pass on defective genes from one generation to the next. Chis have a few defects and problems that show up more often in the breed, and you should be aware of them. Conscientious show breeders test their stock and don't breed dogs with health problems, but sometimes diseases pop up anyway.

Anesthesia Sensitivity

Some Chi owners worry about letting their dogs go under anesthesia for any kind of surgery or procedure, because their little systems are so delicate that if too much anesthesia is given, they can go into shock and die. Fortunately, modern anesthesia techniques have improved and surgery is much safer today than it once was. If the dog is weighed correctly and isn't too frightened, new non-barbiturate anesthesias are much safer.

Bladder Stones

Stones may be caused by a bladder infection or abnormal excretion of minerals by the kidneys. The signs may include frequent urination, straining or inability to urinate, and blood in the urine. If you notice any of these, contact your veterinarian immediately.

Collapsing Trachea

This condition occurs in many small dogs 5 years and older. The dog's windpipe (trachea) narrows or begins to collapse. If your Chi develops a harsh, dry cough, has shortness of breath, and seems exhausted, contact your veterinarian immediately. This is a sign of a collapsing trachea and your Chi may need medication to manage the condition or surgery to repair it.

Heart Problems

Chihuahuas may have heart disease. Pulmonic stenosis and heart murmurs are the most common, particularly in toy breeds. In a dog with pulmonic stenosis, the connection narrows between the heart's right ventricle and the pulmonary artery. This hampers the ability of the right ventricle to pump blood, so the heart muscle thickens.

Heart murmurs occur when the valves don't close completely after each heartbeat and a small amount of blood leaks backward. Murmurs can be detected in young puppies but sometimes disappear as the dog ages. Your veterinarian should monitor your Chi's heart throughout her lifetime and prescribe medication, if it is needed.

It's important to be aware of what health problems occur more often in Chihuahuas, so you can recognize them and get early treatment.

You'll have to carefully observe your Chi for any signs of heart disease, because they are barely noticeable. Persistent coughing, fatigue, fainting, and loss of appetite may signal a problem, especially as it becomes more severe. Your veterinarian can detect the problem by listening to your dog's heart with a stethoscope.

Hydrocephalus

This ailment is sometimes called water on the brain. The head may be excessively large, usually due to swelling. Other symptoms are unsteadiness when walking, frequent falling, eyes that look in opposite directions (also known as east-west eyes), lots of white showing around the eyeballs, and seizures. Puppies or adults with these symptoms usually do not live long. If a Chihuahua shows all the signs of hydrocephalus, it is more humane to have the dog euthanized than to make her endure a limited life span with this painful condition.

Puppies have a hard time storing energy and may suffer from low blood sugar.

Hypoglycemia

Low blood sugar levels in the blood cause hypoglycemia. It occurs most often in very young puppies. Because they have a hard time storing glycogen (a form of sugar) in the liver, sugar levels fluctuate. One way to maintain your Chi puppy's blood sugar level is to feed her several small meals a day until she's about 6 months old. Often a puppy will outgrow the condition and live a perfectly normal life.

The symptoms are weakness, unsteady gait, seizures that may end in loss of consciousness, blindness, and occasionally death. Sometimes the symptoms last only a few seconds, although they may last as long as several minutes. If your puppy faints, put some Karo syrup or honey on her tongue or inside the lips and she will revive. Notify your veterinarian immediately.

Impacted Anal Glands

Impacted anal glands may be a problem. If you see your Chihuahua constantly scooting her rear end along the ground or constantly licking herself around the anus, the anal glands may be impacted. A diet without enough fiber can cause the problem. To add more fiber, try mixing a teaspoon or two of canned pumpkin in with your Chi's regular food once a day.

If your Chi is still having a problem, ask your veterinarian to show you how to empty these sacs; otherwise, a trip to the veterinarian may be needed about every six months to take care of this problem. If the anal sacs aren't emptied regularly, infection may occur and surgery may be required.

Molera

The molera, also called the fontanel, is a soft spot at the top of the skull where the bones have not yet fused, very similar to a baby's soft spot. In a puppy, the molera is enlarged and will gradually grow smaller as the puppy matures, although it may never completely disappear. Sometimes the skull will close completely as a puppy grows, although usually it does not. If it remains about the size of a dime, there is nothing to worry about; just be gentle while patting the skull.

The molera is *not* a defect in the breed, but a unique *characteristic* of the breed. As far as we know, the Chihuahua is the only breed that may have this trait and still be a perfectly healthy dog. According to the breed standard, the Chihuahua may or may not have a molera; 80 percent to 90 percent of Chihuahuas do.

If the molera is large on the skull of an adult or a puppy, there may be a health problem related to hydrocephalus, especially if an excessively large molera is accompanied by other symptoms.

Pancreatitis

Inflammation of the pancreas may occur after the Chihuahua has eaten garbage or has had a fatty meal. Signs include lethargy, loss of appetite, vomiting, diarrhea, and an upset stomach.

Patella Luxation

This condition, also known as slipping stifles, occurs when the patella (kneecap) does not glide smoothly along the groove at the lower end of the femur (the large bone in the thigh). If the groove is too shallow, the patella will pop out when the knee is bent. Patella luxation is common in many small breeds.

During annual checkups your veterinarian can check your Chi's patellas and grade them on a scale of 1 to 4, with 1 being minor and 4 being severe. Surgery can correct abnormalities that are 3's or 4's. Surgery is not recommended in minor cases because the dog will be able to live a relatively normal life, although she may not be an active jumper. Arthritis may develop as the dog ages, but it is apt to occur even in dogs with perfectly normal kneecaps.

Retained Deciduous Teeth

Normally dogs will lose their baby teeth to make room for permanent teeth. In some Chihuahuas the baby teeth don't fall out, and this displaces or obstructs the permanent teeth. Retained baby teeth and the new permanent teeth are so crowded that food becomes trapped. To prevent periodontal disease, your veterinarian will need to remove any baby teeth that don't fall out on their own.

Common Canine Health Problems

What constitutes an emergency? When should you call your veterinarian? If your Chi has difficulty breathing, an allergic reaction, shock, paralysis, uncontrollable bleeding, a broken limb, bloat, urinary obstruction, seizures, uncontrollable diarrhea, or is vomiting, contact your veterinarian or emergency clinic immediately.

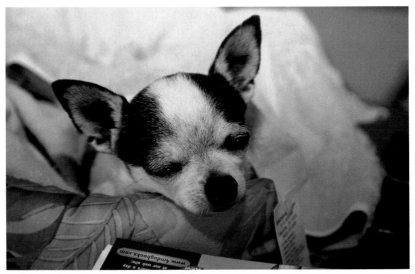

Lethargy and loss of appetite are signs of a sick dog.

Although the list of conditions that could be considered emergencies seems long, most don't happen very often. It's important to know what you can safely treat at home and what the emergencies are. Of course, if you're ever in doubt, call the vet or emergency care facility.

Appetite Loss

A Chihuahua will sometimes refuse to eat for a day or two. If the dog appears to be active, is drinking a normal amount of water, is sleeping as usual, and appears to be normal in every other respect, there is most likely nothing to worry about. If there are other symptoms, such as looking at the water in the bowl but not drinking, lethargy, vomiting, or diarrhea, get immediate veterinary care.

Broken Bones

A Chihuahua's tiny body needs special attention. Their little bones are so small that it's very easy for them to be injured. Always know where your dog is so that she doesn't get stepped on, dropped, or slammed in the door. Leaping off beds or furniture is a definite no-no! One bad landing can easily break bones in the legs or forearms.

If your dog is unable to move a limb, chances are it's broken or she has a spinal injury. You'll need to transport her to the veterinarian immediately. To do so, slowly place her on a blanket or a board, trying not to jar her body.

If you're afraid she will bite you while you're trying to help her, use a length of gauze bandage, a scarf, a bandana, or whatever is handy to make a muzzle. Wrap the cloth around the dog's muzzle twice, cross the ends under her chin, and then pull them behind the dog's ears and tie them securely. Make sure the muzzle restraint is not too tight and that the dog can breathe easily. She should be able to open her mouth a little. Keep the dog covered with a lightweight blanket.

You need to take care when you have a tiny dog; bones are easily broken.

When to Call the Veterinarian

Go to the vet right away or take your dog to an emergency veterinary clinic if:

- Your dog is choking
- Your dog is having trouble breathing
- Your dog has been injured and you cannot stop the bleeding within a few minutes
- Your dog has been stung or bitten by an insect and the site is swelling
- Your dog has been bitten by a snake
- Your dog has been bitten by another animal (including a dog) and shows any swelling or bleeding
- Your dog has touched, licked, or in any way been exposed to a poison
- Your dog has been burned by either heat or caustic chemicals
- Your dog has been hit by a car
- Your dog has any obvious broken bones or cannot put any weight on one of her limbs
- Your dog has a seizure

Make an appointment to see the vet as soon as possible if:

- Your dog has been bitten by a cat, another dog, or a wild animal
- Your dog has been injured and is still limping an hour later

Choking

Puppies are curious creatures and will naturally chew anything they can get into their mouths, be it a bone, a twig, stones, tiny toys, string, or anything else. These can get caught in the teeth or, worse, lodged in the throat and may finally rest in the stomach or intestines. Symptoms may include drooling, pawing at the mouth, gagging, difficulty breathing, blue tongue or mouth, difficulty swallowing, and bloody vomit. If you can see the foreign object and can easily remove it, do so. Otherwise, rush to the veterinarian; surgery may be necessary to save your Chihuahua's life.

- Your dog has unexplained swelling or redness
- Your dog's appetite changes
- Your dog vomits repeatedly and can't seem to keep food down, or drools excessively while eating
- You see any changes in your dog's urination or defecation (pain during elimination, change in regular habits, blood in urine or stool, diarrhea, foul-smelling stool)
- Your dog scoots her rear end on the floor
- Your dog's energy level, attitude, or behavior changes for no apparent reason
- Your dog has crusty or cloudy eyes, or excessive tearing or discharge
- Your dog's nose is dry or chapped, hot, crusty, or runny
- Your dog's ears smell foul, have a dark discharge, or seem excessively waxy
- Your dog's gums are inflamed or bleeding, her teeth look brown, or her breath is foul
- Your dog's skin is red, flaky, itchy, or inflamed, or she keeps chewing at certain spots
- Your dog's coat is dull, dry, brittle, or bare in spots
- Your dog's paws are red, swollen, tender, cracked, or the nails are split or too long
- Your dog is panting excessively, wheezing, unable to catch her breath, breathing heavily, or sounds strange when she breathes

Diarrhea

Diarrhea can be very serious or can simply indicate an upset stomach. If your Chihuahua has no other symptoms and has recovered in a day, she probably just ate something strange.

However, in very small puppies diarrhea can lead to dehydration and death, so obtain medical treatment as quickly as possible. To test your dog for dehydration, take some of her skin between your thumb and forefinger and gently lift the skin upward. If the skin does not go back to its original position quickly, the Chihuahua may be suffering from dehydration. Consult your veterinarian immediately.

Chihuahuas, with their slightly protruding eyes, are prone to eye injuries.

Diarrhea can be caused by many things. Two of the most serious causes are canine parvovirus and canine coronavirus. If diarrhea continues for more than twenty-four hours, if it is bloody, or if you notice other symptoms, call your veterinarian immediately.

Eye Injuries

Because of their slightly protruding eyes, Chihuahuas can be prone to eye injuries. If your Chi injures an eye, flush it out for several minutes using water or a saline solution. This treatment may be sufficient, but if not, transport the dog to a hospital.

Heatstroke

Heatstroke can quickly lead to death. *Never* leave your dog in a car, even with the windows open, even on a cloudy day with the car under the shade of a tree. Heat builds up quickly; your dog could die in a matter of minutes. Do not leave your Chihuahua outside on a hot day without providing shade and fresh water.

How to Make a Canine First-Aid Kit

If your dog hurts herself, even a minor cut, it can be very upsetting for both of you. Having a first-aid kit handy will help you to help her, calmly and efficiently. What should be in your canine first-aid kit?

- Antibiotic ointment
- Antiseptic and antibacterial cleansing wipes
- Benadryl
- Cotton-tipped applicators
- Disposable razor
- Elastic wrap bandages
- Extra leash and collar
- First-aid tape of various widths
- Gauze bandage roll
- Gauze pads of different sizes, including eye pads
- Hydrogen peroxide
- Instant cold compress
- Kaopectate tablets or liquid
- Latex gloves
- Lubricating jelly
- Muzzle
- Nail clippers
- Pen, pencil, and paper for notes and directions
- Pepto-Bismol
- Round-ended scissors and pointy scissors
- Safety pins
- Sterile saline eyewash
- Thermometer (rectal)
- Tweezers

Heatstroke symptoms include collapse, high fever, diarrhea, vomiting, excessive panting, and grayish lips. If you notice these symptoms, cool your Chi immediately. Try to reduce her body temperature by letting her stand on towels soaked in cold water. Also place cool towels on your dog's inner thighs and on her armpits.

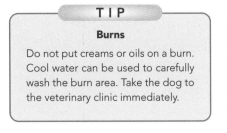

TIP

Burns

Do not put creams or oils on a burn. Cool water can be used to carefully wash the burn area. Take the dog to the veterinary clinic immediately.

Massage the body and legs very gently with a cool towel. Fanning the dog may help. If the dog will drink cool water or chew ice chips, let her. If she won't drink water, wipe the inside of her mouth with cool water or use a water sprayer to spritz a little water into her mouth from the side of her jaw. Also spray water on her inner thighs and armpits. Get the dog to the nearest veterinary hospital right away!

Insect Stings

Stings from bees and other insects are painful and may cause a fatal allergic reaction. Symptoms include swelling around the mouth, face, or body, and difficulty breathing. If a stinger is present, remove it. Clean the swollen area thoroughly with alcohol. Apply a cold compress to reduce swelling and itching and an anti-inflammatory ointment or cream medication. Call your veterinarian

Watch your dog carefully if she has been stung by an insect; bites and stings can cause a serious allergic reaction.

ASPCA Animal Poison Control Center

The ASPCA Animal Poison Control Center has a staff of licensed veterinarians and board-certified toxicologists available 24 hours a day, 365 days a year. The number to call is (888) 426-4435. You will be charged a consultation fee of $50 per case, charged to most major credit cards. There is no charge for follow-up calls in critical cases. At your request, they will also contact your veterinarian. Specific treatment and information can be provided via fax. Put the number in large, legible print with your other emergency telephone numbers. Be prepared to give your name, address, and phone number; what your dog has gotten into (the amount and how long ago); your dog's breed, age, sex, and weight; and what signs and symptoms the dog is showing. You can log onto www.aspca.org and click on "Animal Poison Control Center" for more information, including a list of toxic and nontoxic plants.

immediately and ask if it's okay to give your Chi an antihistamine medication before transporting her to the office for emergency care.

Poisoning

Vomiting, breathing with difficulty, diarrhea, cries of pain, and abnormal body or breath odor are all signs that your pet may have ingested a poisonous substance. Poisons can also be inhaled, absorbed through the skin, or injected into the body. Poisons require professional help without delay! Call the ASPCA Animal Poison Control Center hotline (see the box above), then transport your Chi to your veterinarian or emergency clinic.

Scratches and Cuts

Minor skin irritations, such as scratches, can usually be treated by using an over-the-counter antibiotic cream or ointment. For minor skin problems, many ointments suitable for a baby work well on a Chihuahua.

Part III

Enjoying Your Chihuahua

Chapter 9

Training Your Chihuahua

by Peggy Moran

Training makes your best friend better! A properly trained dog has a happier life and a longer life expectancy. He is also more appreciated by the people he encounters each day, both at home and out and about.

A trained dog walks nicely and joins his family often, going places untrained dogs cannot go. He is never rude or unruly, and he always happily comes when called. When he meets people for the first time, he greets them by sitting and waiting to be petted, rather than jumping up. At home he doesn't compete with his human family, and alone he is not destructive or overly anxious. He isn't continually nagged with words like "no," since he has learned not to misbehave in the first place. He is never shamed, harshly punished, or treated unkindly, and he is a well-loved, involved member of the family.

Sounds good, doesn't it? If you are willing to invest some time, thought, and patience, the words above could soon be used to describe your dog (though perhaps changing "he" to "she"). Educating your pet in a positive way is fun and easy, and there is no better gift you can give your pet than the guarantee of improved understanding and a great relationship.

This chapter will explain how to offer kind leadership, reshape your pet's behavior in a positive and practical way, and even get a head start on simple obedience training.

Understanding Builds the Bond

Dog training is a learning adventure on both ends of the leash. Before attempting to teach their dog new behaviors or change unwanted ones, thoughtful dog owners take the time to understand why their pets behave the way they do, and how their own behavior can be either a positive or negative influence on their dog.

Canine Nature

Loving dogs as much as we do, it's easy to forget they are a completely different species. Despite sharing our homes and living as appreciated members of our families, dogs do not think or learn exactly the same way people do. Even if you love your dog like a child, you must remember to respect the fact that he is actually a dog.

Dogs have no idea when their behavior is inappropriate from a human perspective. They are not aware of the value of possessions they chew or of messes they make or the worry they sometimes seem to cause. While people tend to look at behavior as good and bad or right and wrong, dogs just discover what works and what doesn't work. Then they behave accordingly, learning from their own experiences and increasing or reducing behaviors to improve results for themselves.

You might wonder, "But don't dogs want to please us"? My answer is yes, provided your pleasure reflects back to them in positive ways they can feel and appreciate. Dogs do things for *dog* reasons, and everything they do works for them in some way or they wouldn't be doing it!

The Social Dog

Our pets descended from animals who lived in tightly knit, cooperative social groups. Though far removed in appearance and lifestyle from their ancestors, our dogs still relate in many of the same ways their wild relatives did. And in their relationships with one another, wild canids either lead or follow.

Canine ranking relationships are not about cruelty and power; they are about achievement and abilities. Competent dogs with high levels of drive and confidence step up, while deferring dogs step aside. But followers don't get the short end of the stick; they benefit from the security of having a more competent dog at the helm.

Our domestic dogs still measure themselves against other members of their group—us! Dog owners whose actions lead to positive results have willing, secure followers. But dogs may step up and fill the void or cut loose and do their own thing when their people fail to show capable leadership. When dogs are pushy, aggressive, and rude, or independent and unwilling, it's not because they have designs on the role of "master." It is more likely their owners failed to provide consistent leadership.

Dogs in training benefit from their handler's good leadership. Their education flows smoothly because they are impressed. Being in charge doesn't require you to physically dominate or punish your dog. You simply need to make some subtle changes in the way you relate to him every day.

Lead Your Pack!

Create schedules and structure daily activities. Dogs are creatures of habit and routines will create security. Feed meals at the same times each day and also try to schedule regular walks, training practices, and toilet outings. Your predictability will help your dog be patient.

Ask your dog to perform a task. Before releasing him to food or freedom, have him do something as simple as sit on command. Teach him that cooperation earns great results!

Give a release prompt (such as "let's go") when going through doors leading outside. This is a better idea than allowing your impatient pup to rush past you.

Pet your dog when he is calm, not when he is excited. Turn your touch into a tool that relaxes and settles.

Reward desirable rather than inappropriate behavior. Petting a jumping dog (who hasn't been invited up) reinforces jumping. Pet sitting dogs, and only invite lap dogs up after they've first "asked" by waiting for your invitation.

Replace personal punishment with positive reinforcement. Show a dog what *to do,* and motivate him to want to do it, and there will be no need to punish him for what he should *not do.* Dogs naturally follow, without the need for force or harshness.

Play creatively and appropriately. Your dog will learn the most about his social rank when he is playing with you. During play, dogs work to control toys and try to get the best of one another in a friendly way. The wrong sorts of play can create problems: For example, tug of war can lead to aggressiveness. Allowing your dog to control toys during play may result in possessive guarding when he has something he really values, such as a bone. Dogs who are chased during play may later run away from you when you approach to leash them. The right kinds of play will help increase your dog's social confidence while you gently assert your leadership.

How Dogs Learn (and How They Don't)

Dog training begins as a meeting of minds—yours and your dog's. Though the end goal may be to get your dog's body to behave in a specific way, training starts as a mind game. Your dog is learning all the time by observing the consequences of his actions and social interactions. He is always seeking out what he perceives as desirable and trying to avoid what he perceives as undesirable.

He will naturally repeat a behavior that either brings him more good stuff or makes bad stuff go away (these are both types of reinforcement). He will naturally avoid a behavior that brings him more bad stuff or makes the good stuff go away (these are both types of punishment).

Both reinforcement and punishment can be perceived as either the direct result of something the dog did himself, or as coming from an outside source.

Using Life's Rewards

Your best friend is smart and he is also cooperative. When the best things in life can only be had by working with you, your dog will view you as a facilitator. You unlock doors to all of the positively reinforcing experiences he values: his freedom, his friends at the park, food, affection, walks, and play. The trained dog accompanies you through those doors and waits to see what working with you will bring.

Rewarding your dog for good behavior is called positive reinforcement, and, as we've just seen, it increases the likelihood that he will repeat that behavior. The perfect reward is anything your dog wants that is safe and appropriate. Don't limit yourself to toys, treats, and things that come directly from you. Harness life's positives—barking at squirrels, chasing a falling leaf, bounding away from you at the dog park, pausing for a moment to sniff everything—and allow your dog to earn access to those things as rewards that come from cooperating with you. When he looks at you, when he sits, when he comes when you call—any prompted behavior can earn one of life's rewards. When he works with you, he earns the things he most appreciates; but when he tries to get those things on his own, he cannot. Rather than seeing you as someone who always says "no," your dog will view you as the one who says "let's go!" He will *want* to follow.

What About Punishment?

Not only is it unnecessary to personally punish dogs, it is abusive. No matter how convinced you are that your dog "knows right from wrong," in reality he will associate personal punishment with the punisher. The resulting cowering, "guilty"-looking postures are actually displays of submission and fear. Later,

Purely Positive Reinforcement

With positive training, we emphasize teaching dogs what they should do to earn reinforcements, rather than punishing them for unwanted behaviors.

- Focus on teaching "do" rather than "don't." For example, a sitting dog isn't jumping.
- Use positive reinforcers that are valuable to your dog and the situation: A tired dog values rest; a confined dog values freedom.
- Play (appropriately)!
- Be a consistent leader.
- Set your dog up for success by anticipating and preventing problems.
- Notice and reward desirable behavior, and give him lots of attention when he is being good.
- Train ethically. Use humane methods and equipment that do not frighten or hurt your dog.
- When you are angry, walk away and plan a positive strategy.
- Keep practice sessions short and sweet. Five to ten minutes, three to five times a day is best.

when the punisher isn't around and the coast is clear, the same behavior he was punished for—such as raiding a trash can—might bring a self-delivered, very tasty result. The punished dog hasn't learned not to misbehave; he has learned to not get caught.

Does punishment ever have a place in dog training? Many people will heartily insist it does not. But dog owners often get frustrated as they try to stick to the path of all-positive reinforcement. It sure sounds great, but is it realistic, or even natural, to *never* say "no" to your dog?

A wild dog's life is not *all* positive. Hunger and thirst are both examples of negative reinforcement; the resulting discomfort motivates the wild dog to seek food and water. He encounters natural aversives such as pesky insects; mats in his coat; cold days; rainy days; sweltering hot days; and occasional run-ins with thorns, brambles, skunks, bees, and other nastiness. These all affect his behavior, as he tries to avoid the bad stuff whenever possible. The wild dog also occasionally encounters social punishers from others in his group when he gets too pushy. Starting with a growl or a snap from Mom, and later some mild and ritualized discipline from other members of his four-legged family, he learns to modify behaviors that elicit grouchy responses.

Our pet dogs don't naturally experience all positive results either, because they learn from their surroundings and from social experiences with other dogs. Watch a group of pet dogs playing together and you'll see a very old educational system still being used. As they wrestle and attempt to assert themselves, you'll notice many mouth-on-neck moments. Their playful biting is inhibited, with no intention to cause harm, but their message is clear: "Say uncle or this could hurt more!"

Observing that punishment does occur in nature, some people may feel compelled to try to be like the big wolf with their pet dogs. Becoming aggressive or heavy-handed with your pet will backfire! Your dog will not be impressed, nor will he want to follow you. Punishment causes dogs to change their behavior to avoid or escape discomfort and threats. Threatened dogs will either become very passive and offer submissive, appeasing postures, attempt to flee, or rise to the occasion and fight back. When people personally punish their dogs in an angry manner, one of these three defensive mechanisms will be triggered. Which one depends on a dog's genetic temperament as well as his past social experiences. Since we don't want to make our pets feel the need to avoid or escape us, personal punishment has no place in our training.

Remote Consequences

Sometimes, however, all-positive reinforcement is just not enough. That's because not all reinforcement comes from us. An inappropriate behavior can be self-reinforcing—just doing it makes the dog feel better in some way, whether you are there to say "good boy!" or not. Some examples are eating garbage, pulling the stuffing out of your sofa, barking at passersby, or urinating on the floor.

Although you don't want to personally punish your dog, the occasional deterrent may be called for to help derail these kinds of self-rewarding misbehaviors. In these cases, mild forms of impersonal or remote punishment can be used as part of a correction. The goal isn't to make your dog feel bad or to "know he has done wrong," but to help redirect him to alternate behaviors that are more acceptable to you.

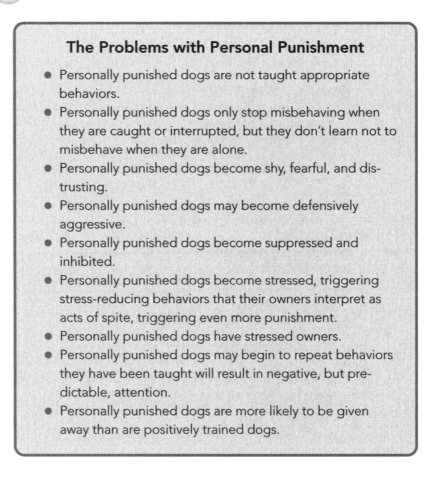

The Problems with Personal Punishment

- Personally punished dogs are not taught appropriate behaviors.
- Personally punished dogs only stop misbehaving when they are caught or interrupted, but they don't learn not to misbehave when they are alone.
- Personally punished dogs become shy, fearful, and distrusting.
- Personally punished dogs may become defensively aggressive.
- Personally punished dogs become suppressed and inhibited.
- Personally punished dogs become stressed, triggering stress-reducing behaviors that their owners interpret as acts of spite, triggering even more punishment.
- Personally punished dogs have stressed owners.
- Personally punished dogs may begin to repeat behaviors they have been taught will result in negative, but predictable, attention.
- Personally punished dogs are more likely to be given away than are positively trained dogs.

You do this by pairing a slightly startling, totally impersonal sound with an equally impersonal and *very mild* remote consequence. The impersonal sound might be a single shake of an empty plastic pop bottle with pennies in it, held out of your dog's sight. Or you could use a vocal expression such as "eh!" delivered with you looking *away* from your misbehaving dog.

Pair your chosen sound—the penny bottle or "eh!"—with either a slight tug on his collar or a sneaky spritz on the rump from a water bottle. Do this right *as* he touches something he should not; bad timing will confuse your dog and undermine your training success.

To keep things under your control and make sure you get the timing right, it's best to do this as a setup. "Accidentally" drop a shoe on the floor, and then help your dog learn some things are best avoided. As he sniffs the shoe say "eh!" without looking at him and give a *slight* tug against his collar. This sound will quickly become meaningful as a correction all by itself—sometimes after just one setup—making the tug correction obsolete. The tug lets your dog see that you were right; going for that shoe *was* a bad idea! Your wise dog will be more likely to heed your warning next time, and probably move closer to you where it's safe. Be a good friend and pick up the nasty shoe. He'll be relieved and you'll look heroic. Later, when he's home alone and encounters a stray shoe, he'll want to give it a wide berth.

Your negative marking sound will come in handy in the future, when your dog begins to venture down the wrong behavioral path. The goal is not to announce your disapproval or to threaten your dog. You are not telling him to stop or showing how *you* feel about his behavior. You are sounding a warning to a friend who's venturing off toward danger—"I wouldn't if I were you!" Suddenly, there is an abrupt, rather startling, noise! Now is the moment to redirect him and help him earn positive reinforcement. That interrupted behavior will become something he wants to avoid in the future, but he won't want to avoid you.

Practical Commands for Family Pets

Before you begin training your dog, let's look at some equipment you'll want to have on hand:

- **A buckle collar** is fine for most dogs. If your dog pulls *very* hard, try a head collar, a device similar to a horse halter that helps reduce pulling by turning the dog's head. *Do not* use a choke chain (sometimes called a training collar), because they cause physical harm even when used correctly.
- **Six-foot training leash and twenty-six–foot retractable leash.**
- **A few empty plastic soda bottles with about twenty pennies in each one.** This will be used to impersonally interrupt misbehaviors before redirecting dogs to more positive activities.
- **A favorite squeaky toy,** to motivate, attract attention, and reward your dog during training.

Lure your dog to take just a few steps with you on the leash by being inviting and enthusiastic. Make sure you reward him for his efforts.

Baby Steps

Allow your young pup to drag a short, lightweight leash attached to a buckle collar for a few *supervised* moments, several times each day. At first the leash may annoy him and he may jump around a bit trying to get away from it. Distract him with your squeaky toy or a bit of his kibble and he'll quickly get used to his new "tail."

Begin walking him on the leash by holding the end and following him. As he adapts, you can begin to assert gentle direct pressure to teach him to follow you. Don't jerk or yank, or he will become afraid to walk when the leash is on. If he becomes hesitant, squat down facing him and let him figure out that by moving toward you he is safe and secure. If he remains confused or frightened and doesn't come to you, go to him and help him understand that you provide safe harbor while he's on the leash. Then back away a few steps and try again to lure him to you. As he learns that you are the "home base," he'll want to follow when you walk a few steps, waiting for you to stop, squat down, and make him feel great.

So Attached to You!

The next step in training your dog—and this is a very important one—is to begin spending at least an hour or more each day with him on a four- to six-foot leash, held by or tethered to you. This training will increase his attachment to you—literally!—as you sit quietly or walk about, tending to your household business. When you are quiet, he'll learn it is time to settle; when you are active, he'll learn to move with you. Tethering also keeps him out of trouble when you are busy but still want his company. It is a great alternative to confining a dog, and can be used instead of crating any time you're home and need to slow him down a bit.

Rotating your dog from supervised freedom to tethered time to some quiet time in the crate or his gated area gives him a diverse and balanced day while he is learning. Two confined or tethered hours is the most you should require of your dog in one stretch, before changing to some supervised freedom, play, or a walk.

The dog in training may, at times, be stressed by all of the changes he is dealing with. Provide a stress outlet, such as a toy to chew on, when he is confined or tethered. He will settle into his quiet time more quickly and completely. Always be sure to provide several rounds of daily play and free time (in a fenced area or on your retractable leash) in addition to plenty of chewing materials.

Dog Talk

Dogs don't speak in words, but they do have a language—body language. They use postures, vocalizations, movements, facial gestures,

Tethering your dog is great way to keep him calm and under control, but still with you.

odors, and touch—usually with their mouths—to communicate what they are feeling and thinking.

We also "speak" using body language. We have quite an array of postures, movements, and facial gestures that accompany our touch and language as we attempt to communicate with our pets. And our dogs can quickly figure us out!

Alone, without associations, words are just noises. But, because we pair them with meaningful body language, our dogs make the connection. Dogs can really learn to understand much of what we *say,* if what we *do* at the same time is consistent.

The Positive Marker

Start your dog's education with one of the best tricks in dog training: Pair various positive reinforcers—food, a toy, touch—with a sound such as a click on a clicker (which you can get at the pet supply store) or a spoken word like "good!" or "yes!" This will enable you to later "mark" your dog's desirable behaviors.

It seems too easy: Just say "yes!" and give the dog his toy. (Or use whatever sound and reward you have chosen.) Later, when you make your marking sound right at the instant your dog does the right thing, he will know you are going to be giving him something good for that particular action. And he'll be eager to repeat the behavior to hear you mark it again!

Next, you must teach your dog to understand the meaning of cues you'll be using to ask him to perform specific behaviors. This is easy, too. Does he already do things you might like him to do on command? Of course! He lies down, he sits, he picks things up, he drops them again, he comes to you. All of the behaviors you'd like to control are already part of your dog's natural repertoire. The trick is getting him to offer those behaviors when you ask for them. And that means you have to teach him to associate a particular behavior on his part with a particular behavior on your part.

Sit Happens

Teach your dog an important new rule: From now on, he is only touched and petted when he is either sitting or lying down. You won't need to ask him to sit; in fact, you should not. Just keeping him tethered near you so there isn't much to do but stand, be ignored, or settle, and wait until sit happens.

He may pester you a bit, but be stoic and unresponsive. Starting now, when *you* are sitting down, a sitting dog is the only one you see and pay attention to. He will eventually sit, and as he does, attach the word "sit"—but don't be too excited or he'll jump right back up. Now mark with your positive sound that promises something good, then reward him with a slow, quiet, settling pet.

Training requires consistent reinforcement. Ask others to also wait until your dog is sitting and calm to touch him, and he will associate being petted with being relaxed. Be sure you train your dog to associate everyone's touch with quiet bonding.

Reinforcing "Sit" as a Command

Since your dog now understands one concept of working for a living—sit to earn petting—you can begin to shape and reinforce his desire to sit. Hold toys, treats, his bowl of food, and turn into a statue. But don't prompt him to sit! Instead, remain frozen and unavailable, looking somewhere out into space, over his head. He will put on a bit of a show, trying to get a response from you, and may offer various behaviors, but only one will push your button—sitting. Wait for him to offer the "right" behavior, and when he does, you unfreeze. Say "sit," then mark with an excited "good!" and give him the toy or treat with a release command—"OK!"

When you notice spontaneous sits occurring, be sure to take advantage of those free opportunities to make your command sequence meaningful and positive. Say "sit" as you observe sit happen—then mark with "good!" and praise, pet, or reward the dog. Soon, every time you look at your dog he'll be sitting and looking right back at you!

Now, after thirty days of purely positive practice, it's time to give him a test. When he is just walking around doing his own thing, suddenly ask him to sit. He'll probably do it right away. If he doesn't, do *not* repeat your command, or you'll just undermine its meaning ("sit" means sit *now;* the command is not "sit, sit, sit, sit"). Instead, get something he likes and let him know you have it. Wait for him to offer the sit—he will—then say "sit!" and complete your marking and rewarding sequence.

OK

"OK" will probably rate as one of your dog's favorite words. It's like the word "recess" to schoolchildren. It is the word used to release your dog from a command. You can introduce "OK" during your "sit" practice. When he gets up from a sit, say "OK" to tell him the sitting is finished. Soon that sound will mean "freedom."

Make it even more meaningful and positive. Whenever he spontaneously bounds away, say "OK!" Squeak a toy, and when he notices and shows interest, toss it for him.

Down

I've mentioned that you should only pet your dog when he is either sitting or lying down. Now, using the approach I've just introduced for "sit," teach your dog to lie down. You will be a statue, and hold something he would like to get but that you'll only release to a dog who is lying down. It helps to lower the desired item to the floor in front of him, still not speaking and not letting him have it until he offers you the new behavior you are seeking.

Lower your dog's reward to the floor to help him figure out what behavior will earn him his reward.

He may offer a sit and then wait expectantly, but you must make him keep searching for the new trick that triggers your generosity. Allow your dog to experiment and find the right answer, even if he has to search around for it first. When he lands on "down" and learns it is another behavior that works, he'll offer it more quickly the next time.

Don't say "down" until he lies down, to tightly associate your prompt with the correct behavior. To say "down, down, down" as he is sitting, looking at you, or pawing at the toy would make "down" mean those behaviors instead! Whichever behavior he offers, a training opportunity has been created. Once you've attached and shaped both sitting and lying down, you can ask for both behaviors with your verbal prompts, "sit" or "down." Be sure to only reinforce the "correct" reply!

Stay

"Stay" can easily be taught as an extension of what you've already been practicing. To teach "stay," you follow the entire sequence for reinforcing a "sit" or "down," except you wait a bit longer before you give the release word, "OK!" Wait a second or two longer during each practice before saying "OK!" and releasing your dog to the positive reinforcer (toy, treat, or one of life's other rewards).

You can step on the leash to help your dog understand the down-stay, but only do this when he is already lying down. You don't want to hurt him!

If he gets up before you've said "OK," you have two choices: pretend the release was your idea and quickly interject "OK!" as he breaks; or, if he is more experienced and practiced, mark the behavior with your correction sound—"eh!"—and then gently put him back on the spot, wait for him to lie down, and begin again. Be sure the next three practices are a success. Ask him to wait for just a second, and release him before he can be wrong. You need to keep your dog feeling like more of a success than a failure as you begin to test his training in increasingly more distracting and difficult situations.

As he gets the hang of it—he stays until you say "OK"—you can gradually push for longer times—up to a minute on a sit-stay, and up to three minutes on a down-stay. You can also gradually add distractions and work in new environments. To add a minor self-correction for the down-stay, stand on the dog's leash after he lies down, allowing about three inches of slack. If tries to get up before you've said "OK," he'll discover it doesn't work.

Do not step on the leash to make your dog lie down! This could badly hurt his neck, and will destroy his trust in you. Remember, we are teaching our dogs to make the best choices, not inflicting our answers upon them!

Come

Rather than thinking of "come" as an action—"come to me"—think of it as a place—"the dog is sitting in front of me, facing me." Since your dog by now really likes sitting to earn your touch and other positive reinforcement, he's likely to sometimes sit directly in front of you, facing you, all on his own. When this happens, give it a specific name: "come."

Now follow the rest of the training steps you have learned to make him like doing it and reinforce the behavior by practicing it any chance you get. Anything your dog wants and likes could be earned as a result of his first offering the sit-in-front known as "come."

You can help guide him into the right location. Use your hands as "landing gear" and pat the insides of your legs at his nose level. Do this while backing up a bit, to help him maneuver to the straight-in-front, facing-you position. Don't say the

Pat the insides of your legs to show your dog exactly where you like him to sit when you say "come."

word "come" while he's maneuvering, because he hasn't! You are trying to make "come" the end result, not the work in progress.

You can also help your dog by marking his movement in the right direction: Use your positive sound or word to promise he is getting warm. When he finally sits facing you, enthusiastically say "come," mark again with your positive word, and release him with an enthusiastic "OK!" Make it so worth his while, with lots of play and praise, that he can't wait for you to ask him to come again!

Building a Better Recall

Practice, practice, practice. Now, practice some more. Teach your dog that all good things in life hinge upon him first sitting in front of you in a behavior named "come." When you think he really has got it, test him by asking him to "come" as you gradually add distractions and change locations. Expect setbacks as you make these changes and practice accordingly. Lower your expectations and make his task easier so he is able to get it right. Use those distractions as rewards, when they are appropriate. For example, let him check out the interesting leaf that blew by as a reward for first coming to you and ignoring it.

Add distance and call your dog to come while he is on his retractable leash. If he refuses and sits looking at you blankly, *do not* jerk, tug, "pop," or reel him in. Do nothing! It is his move; wait to see what behavior he offers. He'll either begin to approach (mark the behavior with an excited "good!"), sit and do nothing (just keep waiting), or he'll try to move in some direction other than toward you. If he tries to leave, use your correction marker—"eh!"—and bring him to a stop by letting him walk to the end of the leash, *not* by jerking him. Now walk to him in a neutral manner, and don't jerk or show any disapproval. Gently bring him back to the spot where he was when you called him, then back away and face him, still waiting and not reissuing your command. Let him keep examining his options until he finds the one that works—yours!

If you have practiced everything I've suggested so far and given your dog a chance to really learn what "come" means, he is well aware of what you want and is quite intelligently weighing all his options. The only way he'll know your way is the one that works is to be allowed to examine his other choices and discover that they *don't* work.

Sooner or later every dog tests his training. Don't be offended or angry when your dog tests you. No matter how positive you've made it, he won't always want to do everything you ask, every time. When he explores the "what happens if I don't" scenario, your training is being strengthened. He will discover through his own process of trial and error that the best—and only—way out of a command he really doesn't feel compelled to obey is to obey it.

Let's Go

Many pet owners wonder if they can retain control while walking their dogs and still allow at least some running in front, sniffing, and playing. You might worry that allowing your dog occasional freedom could result in him expecting it all the time, leading to a testy, leash-straining walk. It's possible for both parties on the leash to have an enjoyable experience by implementing and reinforcing well-thought-out training techniques.

Begin by making word associations you'll use on your walks. Give the dog some slack on the leash, and as he starts to walk away from you say "OK" and begin to follow him.

Do not let him drag you; set the pace even when he is being given a turn at being the leader. Whenever he starts to pull, just come to a standstill and refuse to move (or refuse to allow him to continue forward) until there is slack in the leash. Do this correction without saying anything at all. When he isn't pulling, you may decide to just stand still and let him sniff about within the range the slack leash allows, or you may even mosey along following him. After a few minutes of "recess," it is time to work. Say something like "that's it" or "time's up," close the distance between you and your dog, and touch him.

Next say "let's go" (or whatever command you want to use to mean "follow me as we walk"). Turn and walk off, and, if he follows, mark his behavior with "good!" Then stop,

Give your dog slack on his leash as you walk and let him make the decision to walk with you.

When your dog catches up with you, make sure you let him know what a great dog he is!

Intersperse periods of attentive walking, where your dog is on a shorter leash, with periods on a slack leash, where he is allowed to look and sniff around.

squat down, and let him catch you. Make him glad he did! Start again, and do a few transitions as he gets the hang of your follow-the-leader game, speeding up, slowing down, and trying to make it fun. When you stop, he gets to catch up and receive some deserved positive reinforcement. Don't forget that's the reason he is following you, so be sure to make it worth his while!

Require him to remain attentive to you. Do not allow sniffing, playing, eliminating, or pulling during your time as leader on a walk. If he seems to get distracted—which, by the way, is the main reason dogs walk poorly with their people— change direction or pace without saying a word. Just help him realize "oops, I lost track of my human." Do not jerk his neck and say "heel"—this will make the word "heel" mean pain in the neck and will not encourage him to cooperate with you. Don't repeat "let's go," either. He needs to figure out that it is his job to keep track of and follow you if he wants to earn the positive benefits you provide.

The best reward you can give a dog for performing an attentive, controlled walk is a few minutes of walking without all of the controls. Of course, he must remain on a leash even during the "recess" parts of the walk, but allowing him to discriminate between attentive following—"let's go"—and having a few moments of relaxation—"OK"—will increase his willingness to work.

Training for Attention

Your dog pretty much has a one-track mind. Once he is focused on something, everything else is excluded. This can be great, for instance, when he's focusing on you! But it can also be dangerous if, for example, his attention is riveted on the bunny he is chasing and he does not hear you call—that is, not unless he has been trained to pay attention when you say his name.

When you say your dog's name, you'll want him to make eye contact with you. Begin teaching this by making yourself so intriguing that he can't help but look.

When you call your dog's name, you will again be seeking a specific response—eye contact. The best way to teach this is to trigger his alerting response by making a noise with your mouth, such as whistling or a kissing sound, and then immediately doing something he'll find very intriguing.

You can play a treasure hunt game to help teach him to regard his name as a request for attention. As a bonus, you can reinforce the rest of his new vocabulary at the same time.

Treasure Hunt

Make a kissing sound, then jump up and find a dog toy or dramatically raid the fridge and rather noisily eat a piece of cheese. After doing this twice, make a kissing sound and then look at your dog.

Of course he is looking at you! He is waiting to see if that sound—the kissing sound—means you're going to go hunting again. After all, you're so good at it! Because he is looking, say his name, mark with "good," then go hunting and find his toy. Release it to him with an "OK." At any point if he follows you, attach your "let's go!" command; if he leaves you, give permission with "OK."

Using this approach, he cannot be wrong—any behavior your dog offers can be named. You can add things like "take it" when he picks up a toy, and "thank you" when he happens to drop one. Many opportunities to make your new vocabulary meaningful and positive can be found within this simple training game.

Problems to watch out for when teaching the treasure hunt:

- You really do not want your dog to come to you when you call his name (later, when you try to engage his attention to ask him to stay, he'll already be on his way toward you). You just want him to look at you.
- Saying "watch me, watch me" doesn't teach your dog to *offer* his attention. It just makes you a background noise.
- Don't lure your dog's attention with the reward. Get his attention and then reward him for looking. Try holding a toy in one hand with your arm stretched out to your side. Wait until he looks at you rather than the toy. Now say his name then mark with "good!" and release the toy. As he goes for it, say "OK."

To get your dog's attention, try holding his toy with your arm out to your side. Wait until he looks at you, then mark the moment and give him the toy.

Teaching Cooperation

Never punish your dog for failing to obey you or try to punish him into compliance. Bribing, repeating yourself, and doing a behavior for him all avoid the real issue of dog training—his will. He must be helped to be willing, not made to achieve tasks. Good dog training helps your dog want to obey. He learns that he can gain what he values most through cooperation and compliance, and can't gain those things any other way.

Your dog is learning to *earn,* rather than expect, the good things in life. And you've become much more important to him than you were before. Because you are allowing him to experiment and learn, he doesn't have to be forced, manipulated, or bribed. When he wants something, he can gain it by cooperating with you. One of those "somethings"—and a great reward you shouldn't underestimate—is your positive attention, paid to him with love and sincere approval!

Chapter 10

Housetraining Your Chihuahua

Excerpted from Housetraining: An Owner's Guide to a Happy Healthy Pet, 1st Edition, *by September Morn*

By the time puppies are about 3 weeks old, they start to follow their mother around. When they are a few steps away from their clean sleeping area, the mama dog stops. The pups try to nurse but mom won't allow it. The pups mill around in frustration, then nature calls and they all urinate and defecate here, away from their bed. The mother dog returns to the nest, with her brood waddling behind her. Their first housetraining lesson has been a success.

The next one to housetrain puppies should be their breeder. The breeder watches as the puppies eliminate, then deftly removes the soiled papers and replaces them with clean papers before the pups can traipse back through their messes. He has wisely arranged the puppies' space so their bed, food, and drinking water are as far away from the elimination area as possible. This way, when the pups follow their mama, they will move away from their sleeping and eating area before eliminating. This habit will help the pups be easily housetrained.

Your Housetraining Shopping List

While your puppy's mother and breeder are getting her started on good housetraining habits, you'll need to do some shopping. If you have all the essentials in place before your dog arrives, it will be easier to help her learn the rules from day one.

Newspaper: The younger your puppy and larger her breed, the more newspapers you'll need. Newspaper is absorbent, abundant, cheap, and convenient.

Puddle Pads: If you prefer not to stockpile newspaper, a commercial alternative is puddle pads. These thick paper pads can be purchased under several trade names at pet supply stores. The pads have waterproof backing, so puppy urine doesn't seep through onto the floor. Their disadvantages are that they will cost you more than newspapers and that they contain plastics that are not biodegradable.

Poop Removal Tool: There are several types of poop removal tools available. Some are designed with a separate pan and rake, and others have the handles hinged like scissors. Some scoops need two hands for operation, while others are designed for one-handed use. Try out the different brands at your pet supply store. Put a handful of pebbles or dog kibble on the floor and then pick them up with each type of scoop to determine which works best for you.

Plastic Bags: When you take your dog outside your yard, you *must* pick up after her. Dog waste is unsightly, smelly, and can harbor disease. In many cities and towns, the law mandates dog owners clean up pet waste deposited on public ground. Picking up after your dog using a plastic bag scoop is simple. Just put your hand inside the bag, like a mitten, and then grab the droppings. Turn the bag inside out, tie the top, and that's that.

Crate: To housetrain a puppy, you will need some way to confine her when you're unable to supervise. A dog crate is a secure way to confine your dog for short periods during the day and to use as a comfortable bed at night. Crates come in wire mesh and in plastic. The wire ones are foldable to store flat in a smaller space. The plastic ones are more cozy, draft-free, and quiet, and are approved for airline travel.

Baby Gates: Since you shouldn't crate a dog for more than an hour or two at a time during the day, baby gates are a good way to limit your dog's freedom in the house. Be sure the baby gates you use are safe. The old-fashioned wooden, expanding lattice type has seriously injured a number of children by collapsing and trapping a leg, arm, or neck. That type of gate can hurt a puppy, too, so use the modern grid type gates instead. You'll need more than one baby gate if you have several doorways to close off.

Housetraining is a matter of establishing good habits right from the start. The very first day, take your puppy to her elimination spot and praise her when she goes.

Exercise Pen: Portable exercise pens are great when you have a young pup or a small dog. These metal or plastic pens are made of rectangular panels that are hinged together. The pens are freestanding, sturdy, foldable, and can be carried like a suitcase. You could set one up in your kitchen as the pup's daytime corral, and then take it outdoors to contain your pup while you garden or just sit and enjoy the day.

Enzymatic Cleaner: All dogs make housetraining mistakes. Accept this and be ready for it by buying an enzymatic cleaner made especially for pet accidents. Dogs like to eliminate where they have done it before, and lingering smells lead them to those spots. Ordinary household cleaners may remove all the odors you can smell, but only an enzymatic cleaner will remove everything your dog can smell.

The First Day

Housetraining is a matter of establishing good habits in your dog. That means you never want her to learn anything she will eventually have to unlearn. Start off housetraining on the right foot by teaching your dog that you prefer her to eliminate outside. Designate a potty area in your backyard (if you have one) or in the street in front of your home and take your dog to it as soon as you arrive home. Let her sniff a bit and, when she squats to go, give the action a name: "potty" or "do it" or anything else you won't be embarrassed to say in public. Eventually your dog will associate that word with the act and will eliminate on command. When she's finished, praise her with "good potty!"

Don't Overuse the Crate

A crate serves well as a dog's overnight bed, but you should not leave the dog in her crate for more than an hour or two during the day. Throughout the day, she needs to play and exercise. She is likely to want to drink some water and will undoubtedly eliminate. Confining your dog all day will give her no option but to soil her crate. This is not just unpleasant for you and the dog, but it reinforces bad cleanliness habits. And crating a pup for the whole day is abusive. Don't do it.

That first day, take your puppy out to the potty area frequently. Although she may not eliminate every time, you are establishing a routine: You take her to her spot, ask her to eliminate, and praise her when she does.

Just before bedtime, take your dog to her potty area once more. Stand by and wait until she produces. Do not put your dog to bed for the night until she has eliminated. Be patient and calm. This is not the time to play with or excite your dog. If she's too excited, a pup not only won't eliminate, she probably won't want to sleep either.

Most dogs, even young ones, will not soil their beds if they can avoid it. For this reason, a sleeping crate can be a tremendous help during housetraining. Being crated at night can help a dog develop the muscles that control elimination. So after your dog has emptied out, put her to bed in her crate.

A good place to put your dog's sleeping crate is near your own bed. Dogs are pack animals, so they feel safer sleeping with others in a common area. In your bedroom, the pup will be near you and you'll be close enough to hear when she wakes during the night and needs to eliminate.

Pups under 4 months old often are not able to hold their urine all night. If your puppy has settled down to sleep but awakens and fusses a few hours later, she probably needs to go out. For the best housetraining progress, take your pup to her elimination area whenever she needs to go, even in the wee hours of the morning.

Your pup may soil in her crate if you ignore her late night urgency. It's unfair to let this happen, and it sends the wrong message about your expectations for cleanliness. Resign yourself to this midnight outing and just get up and take the pup out. Your pup will outgrow this need soon and will learn in the process that she can count on you, and you'll wake happily each morning to a clean dog.

Your dog's crate will be an important housetraining tool.

The next morning, the very first order of business is to take your pup out to eliminate. Don't forget to take her to her special potty spot, ask her to eliminate, and then praise her when she does. After your pup empties out in the morning, give her breakfast, and then take her to her potty area again. After that, she shouldn't need to eliminate again right away, so you can allow her some free playtime. Keep an eye on the pup though, because when she pauses in play she may need to go potty. Take her to the right spot, give the command, and praise if she produces.

Confine Your Pup

A pup or dog who has not finished housetraining should *never* be allowed the run of the house unattended. A new dog (especially a puppy) with unlimited access to your house will make her own choices about where to eliminate. Vigilance during your new dog's first few weeks in your home will pay big dividends. Every potty mistake delays housetraining progress; every success speeds it along.

Prevent problems by setting up a controlled environment for your new pet. A good place for a puppy corral is often the kitchen. Kitchens almost always have waterproof or easily cleaned floors, which is a distinct asset with leaky pups. A bathroom, laundry room, or enclosed porch could be used for a puppy corral, but the kitchen is generally the best location. Kitchens are a meeting place and a hub of activity for many families, and a puppy will learn better manners when she is socialized thoroughly with family, friends, and nice strangers.

The way you structure your pup's corral area is very important. Her bed, food, and water should be at the opposite end of the corral from the potty area. When you first get your pup, spread newspaper over the rest of the floor of her playpen corral. Lay the papers at least four pages thick and be sure to overlap the edges. As you note the pup's progress, you can remove the papers nearest the sleeping and eating corner. Gradually decrease the size of the papered area until only the end where you want the pup to eliminate is covered. If you will be training your dog to eliminate outside, place newspaper at the end of the corral that is closest to the door that leads outdoors. That way as she moves away from the clean area to the papered area, the pup will also form the habit of heading toward the door to go out.

Maintain a scent marker for the pup's potty area by reserving a small soiled piece of paper when you clean up. Place this piece, with her scent of urine, under the top sheet of the clean papers you spread. This will cue your pup where to eliminate.

Most dog owners use a combination of indoor papers and outdoor elimination areas. When the pup is left by herself in the corral, she can potty on the ever-present newspaper. When you are available to take the pup outside, she can do her business in the outdoor spot. It is not difficult to switch a pup from indoor paper training to outdoor elimination. Owners of large pups often switch early, but potty papers are still useful if the pup spends time in her indoor corral while you're away. Use the papers as long as your pup needs them. If you come home and they haven't been soiled, you are ahead.

> ### T I P
>
> **Water**
>
> Make sure your dog has access to clean water at all times. Limiting the amount of water a dog drinks is not necessary for housetraining success and can be very dangerous. A dog needs water to digest food, to maintain a proper body temperature and proper blood volume, and to clean her system of toxins and wastes. A healthy dog will automatically drink the right amount. Do not restrict water intake. Controlling your dog's access to water is not the key to housetraining her; controlling her access to everything else in your home is.

When setting up your pup's outdoor yard, put the lounging area as far away as possible from the potty area, just as with the indoor corral setup. People with large yards, for example, might leave a patch unmowed at the edge of the lawn to serve as the dog's elimination area. Other dog owners teach the dog to relieve herself in a designated corner of a deck or patio. For an apartment-dwelling city dog, the outdoor potty area might be a tiny balcony or the curb. Each dog owner has somewhat different expectations for their dog. Teach your dog to eliminate in a spot that suits your environment and lifestyle.

Be sure to pick up droppings in your yard at least once a day. Dogs have a natural desire to stay far away from their own excrement, and if too many piles litter the ground, your dog won't want to walk through it and will start eliminating elsewhere. Leave just one small piece of feces in the potty area to remind your dog where the right spot is located.

To help a pup adapt to the change from indoors to outdoors, take one of her potty papers outside to the new elimination area. Let the pup stand on the paper

Take your pup to her outdoor potty place frequently throughout the day. Keep her leashed so she won't just wander around.

when she goes potty outdoors. Each day for four days, reduce the size of the paper by half. By the fifth day, the pup, having used a smaller and smaller piece of paper to stand on, will probably just go to that spot and eliminate.

Take your pup to her outdoor potty place frequently throughout the day. A puppy can hold her urine for only about as many hours as her age in months, and will move her bowels as many times a day as she eats. So a 2-month-old pup will urinate about every two hours, while at 4 months she can manage about four hours between piddles. Pups vary somewhat in their rate of development, so this is not a hard and fast rule. It does, however, present a realistic idea of how long a pup can be left without access to a potty place. Past 4 months, her potty trips will be less frequent.

When you take the dog outdoors to her spot, keep her leashed so that she won't wander away. Stand quietly and let her sniff around in the designated area. If your pup starts to leave before she has eliminated, gently lead her back and remind her to go. If your pup sniffs at the spot, praise her calmly, say the command word, and just wait. If she produces, praise serenely, then give her time to sniff around a little more. She may not be finished, so give her time to go again before allowing her to play and explore her new home.

If you find yourself waiting more than five minutes for your dog to potty, take her back inside. Watch your pup carefully for twenty minutes, not giving her any opportunity to slip away to eliminate unnoticed. If you are too busy to watch the pup, put her in her crate. After twenty minutes, take her to the outdoor potty spot again and tell her what to do. If you're unsuccessful after five minutes, crate the dog again. Give her another chance to eliminate in fifteen or twenty minutes. Eventually, she will have to go.

Watch Your Pup

Be vigilant and don't let the pup make a mistake in the house. Each time you successfully anticipate elimination and take your pup to the potty spot, you'll move a step closer to your goal. Stay aware of your puppy's needs. If you ignore the pup, she will make mistakes and you'll be cleaning up more messes.

Keep a chart of your new dog's elimination behavior for the first three or four days. Jot down what times she eats, sleeps, and eliminates. After several days a pattern will emerge that can help you determine your pup's body rhythms. Most dogs tend to eliminate at fairly regular intervals. Once you know your new dog's natural rhythms, you'll be able to anticipate her needs and schedule appropriate potty outings.

Understanding the meanings of your dog's postures can also help you win the battle of the puddle. When your dog is getting ready to eliminate, she will display a specific set of postures. The sooner you can learn to read these signals, the cleaner your floor will stay.

A young puppy who feels the urge to eliminate may start to sniff the ground and walk in a circle. If the pup is very young, she may simply squat and go. All young puppies, male or female, squat to urinate. If you are housetraining a pup under 4 months of age, regardless of sex, watch for the beginnings of a squat as the signal to rush the pup to the potty area.

When a puppy is getting ready to defecate, she may run urgently

Try not to let your pup make a mistake in the house. Be alert to her signals that she needs to go out and pick her up and take her out before she has an accident.

back and forth or turn in a circle while sniffing or starting to squat. If defecation is imminent, the pup's anus may protrude or open slightly. When she starts to go, the pup will squat and hunch her back, her tail sticking straight out behind. There is no mistaking this posture; nothing else looks like this. If your pup takes this position, take her to her potty area. Hurry! You may have to carry her to get there in time.

A young puppy won't have much time between feeling the urge and actually eliminating, so you'll have to be quick to note her postural clues and intercept your pup in time. Pups from 3 to 6 months have a few seconds more between the urge and the act than younger ones do. The older your pup, the more time you'll have to get her to the potty area after she begins the posture signals that alert you to her need.

Accidents Happen

If you see your pup about to eliminate somewhere other than the designated area, interrupt her immediately. Say "wait, wait, wait!" or clap your hands loudly to startle her into stopping. Carry the pup, if she's still small enough, or take her collar and lead her to the correct area. Once your dog is in the potty area, give her the command to eliminate. Use a friendly voice for the command, then wait patiently for her to produce. The pup may be tense because you've just startled her and may have to relax a bit before she's able to eliminate. When she does her job, include the command word in the praise you give ("good potty").

The old-fashioned way of housetraining involved punishing a dog's mistakes even before she knew what she was supposed to do. Puppies were punished for breaking rules they didn't understand about functions they couldn't control. This was not fair. While your dog is new to housetraining, there is no need or excuse for punishing her mistakes. Your job is to take the dog to the potty area just before she needs to go, especially with pups under 3 months old. If you aren't watching your pup closely enough and she has an accident, don't punish the puppy for your failure to anticipate her needs. It's not the pup's fault; it's yours.

In any case, punishment is not an effective tool for housetraining most dogs. Many will react to punishment by hiding puddles and feces where you won't find them right away (like behind the couch or under the desk). This eventually may lead to punishment after the fact, which leads to more hiding, and so on.

Instead of punishing for mistakes, stay a step ahead of potty accidents by learning to anticipate your pup's needs. Accompany your dog to the designated potty area when she needs to go. Tell her what you want her to do and praise her when she goes. This will work wonders. Punishment won't be necessary if you are a good teacher.

A baby puppy does not have the physical ability to control her bladder and bowels for very long. Please don't expect more from your dog than she can do.

What happens if you come upon a mess after the fact? Some trainers say a dog can't remember having eliminated, even a few moments after she has done so. This is not true. The fact is that urine and feces carry a dog's unique scent, which she (and every other dog) can instantly recognize. So, if you happen upon a potty mistake after the fact you can still use it to teach your dog.

But remember, no punishment! Spanking, hitting, shaking, or scaring a puppy for having a housetraining accident is confusing and counterproductive. Spend your energy instead on positive forms of teaching.

Take your pup and a paper towel to the mess. Point to the urine or feces and calmly tell your puppy, "no potty here." Then scoop or sop up the accident with the paper towel. Take the evidence and the pup to the approved potty area. Drop the mess on the ground and tell the dog, "good potty here," as if she had done the deed in the right place. If your pup sniffs at the evidence, praise her calmly. If the accident happened very recently your dog may not have to go yet, but wait with her a few minutes anyway. If she eliminates, praise her. Afterwards, go finish cleaning up the mess.

Soon the puppy will understand that there is a place where you are pleased about elimination and other places where you are not. Praising for elimination in the approved place will help your pup remember the rules.

Scheduling Basics

With a new puppy in the home, don't be surprised if your rising time is suddenly a little earlier than you've been accustomed to. Puppies have earned a reputation as very early risers. When your pup wakes you at the crack of dawn, you will have to get up and take her to her elimination spot. Be patient. When your dog is an adult, she may enjoy sleeping in as much as you do.

At the end of the chapter, you'll find a typical housetraining schedule for puppies aged 10 weeks to 6 months. (To find schedules for younger and older pups, and for adult dogs, visit this book's companion Web site.) It's fine to adjust the rising times when using this schedule, but you should not adjust the intervals between feedings and potty outings unless your pup's behavior justifies a change. Your puppy can only meet your expectations in housetraining if you help her learn the rules.

The schedule for puppies is devised with the assumption that someone will be home most of the time with the pup. That would be the best scenario, of course, but is not always possible. You may be able to ease the problems of a latchkey pup by having a neighbor or friend look in on the pup at noon and take her to eliminate. A better solution might be hiring a pet sitter to drop by midday. A professional pet sitter will be knowledgeable about companion animals and can give your pup high-quality care and socialization. Some can even

Housetraining may seem like it takes up all your time at first. But as your dog gets older, she will learn to control herself and you'll be able to schedule fewer walks.

help train your pup in both potty manners and basic obedience. Ask your veterinarian and your dog-owning friends to recommend a good pet sitter.

If you must leave your pup alone during her early housetraining period, be sure to cover the entire floor of her corral with thick layers of overlapping newspaper. If you come home to messes in the puppy corral, just clean them up. Be patient—she's still a baby.

Use this schedule (and the ones on the companion Web site) as a basic plan to help prevent housetraining accidents. Meanwhile, use your own powers of observation to discover how to best modify the basic schedule to fit your dog's unique needs. Each dog is an individual and will have her own rhythms, and each dog is reliable at a different age.

Schedule for Pups 10 Weeks to 6 Months

7:00 a.m.	Get up and take the puppy from her sleeping crate to her potty spot.
7:15	Clean up last night's messes, if any.
7:30	Food and fresh water.
7:45	Pick up the food bowl. Take the pup to her potty spot; wait and praise.
8:00	The pup plays around your feet while you have your breakfast.
9:00	Potty break (younger pups may not be able to wait this long).
9:15	Play and obedience practice.
10:00	Potty break.
10:15	The puppy is in her corral with safe toys to chew and play with.
11:30	Potty break (younger pups may not be able to wait this long).
11:45	Food and fresh water.
12:00 p.m.	Pick up the food bowl and take the pup to her potty spot.
12:15	The puppy is in her corral with safe toys to chew and play with.
1:00	Potty break (younger pups may not be able to wait this long).

continues

Schedule for Pups 10 Weeks to 6 Months *(continued)*

1:15	Put the pup on a leash and take her around the house with you.
3:30	Potty break (younger pups may not be able to wait this long).
3:45	Put the pup in her corral with safe toys and chews for solitary play and/or a nap.
4:45	Potty break.
5:00	Food and fresh water.
5:15	Potty break.
5:30	The pup may play nearby (either leashed or in her corral) while you prepare your evening meal.
7:00	Potty break.
7:15	Leashed or closely watched, the pup may play and socialize with family and visitors.
9:15	Potty break (younger pups may not be able to wait this long).
10:45	Last chance to potty.
11:00	Put the pup to bed in her crate for the night.

Appendix

Learning More About Your Chihuahua

Some Good Books

Andrews, Barbara J., *Chihuahua*, Interpet Publishing, 2000.
O'Neil, Jacqueline, *Chihuahuas For Dummies*, Wiley Publishing, 2000.

Care and Health

Arden, Darlene, *The Angell Memorial Animal Hospital Book of Wellness & Preventive Care for Dogs*, McGraw-Hill, 2002.
Arden, Darlene, *Small Dogs, Big Hearts: A Guide to Caring for Your Little Dog*, Howell Book House, 2006.
Bamberger, Michelle, DVM, *Help! The Quick Guide to First Aid for Your Dog*, Howell Book House, 1995.
Messonnier, Shawn, *DVM, Natural Health Bible for Dogs & Cats: You're A–Z Guide to Over 200 Conditions, Herbs, Vitamins, and Supplements*, Three Rivers Press, 2001.

Training

Benjamin, Carol Lea, *Mother Knows Best,* Howell Book House, 1985.
Kalstone, Shirlee, *How to Housebreak Your Dog in Seven Days*, Revised Edition, Bantam Books, 2004.
McConnell, Patricia, *The Other End of the Leash,* Ballantine Books, 2003.
Smith, Cheryl S., *The Rosetta Bone,* Howell Book House, 2004.

Canine Activities

Cecil, Barbara, and Gerianne Darnell, *Competitive Obedience Training for the Small Dog*, T9E Publishing, 1994.

Davis, Kathy Diamond, *Therapy Dogs: Training Your Dog to Help Others*, 2nd Edition, Dogwise Publications, 2002.

Mobil Travel Guide, *On the Road with Your Pet*, Mobil Travel Guides, 2004.

Simmons-Moake, Jane, *Agility Training: The Fun Sport for All Dogs*, Howell Book House, 1991.

Smith, Cheryl S., *The Absolute Beginner's Guide to Showing Your Dog*, Three Rivers Press, 2001.

Volhard, Jack and Wendy, *The Canine Good Citizen: Every Dog Can Be One*, 2nd Edition, Howell Book House, 1997.

Magazines

AKC Gazette
AKC Family Dog
American Kennel Club
260 Madison Avenue
New York, NY 10016
(212) 696-8200
www.akc.org

The Bark
2810 8th Street
Berkeley, CA 94710
(510) 704-0827
www.thebark.com

Los Chihuahuas Magazine
12860 Rhonotosassa Road
Dover, Florida 33527
(813) 986-2943

Dog Fancy
P.O. Box 37185
Boone, IA 50037-0185
(800) 896-4939
www.dogfancy.com

Top Notch Toys
Doll-McGinnis Enterprises
8848 Beverly Hills
Lakeland, FL 33809
(813) 858-3839
www.dmcg.com

Clubs and Registries

There are numerous all-breed, individual breed, canine sport, and other special-interest dog clubs across the country. The American Kennel Club can provide you with a list of clubs in your area.

American Kennel Club (AKC)
260 Madison Avenue
New York, NY 10016
www.akc.org
In addition to the informative main Web site, there are special links to AKC affiliates such as Companion Animal Recovery (CAR) and the Canine Health Foundation (CHF). The AKC produces a video on every dog breed and also produces many informative pamphlets, videos, and books.

Canadian Kennel Club (CKC)
89 Skyway Avenue
Etobicoke, Ontario
Canada M9W 6R4
(800) 250-8040 or (416) 675-5511
www.ckc.ca

United Kennel Club (UKC)
100 E. Kilgore Road
Kalamazoo, MI 49001-5598
(616) 343-9020
www.ukcdogs.com

Web Sites

Chihuahua Club of America
www.chihuahuaclubofamerica.com
The club can send you information on all aspects of the breed, including the names and addresses of breed clubs in your area, as well as obedience clubs. They also have a *Chihuahua Handbook*, which includes articles about the breed, the club's history, and pedigree information.

Veterinary Organizations

American Animal Hospital Association
www.healthypet.com
Information on pet health and ownership trends.

American Holistic Veterinary Medicine Association
www.ahvma.org
Information on holistic care, and a search feature to help you find practitioners in your area.

American Veterinary Medical Association
www.avma.org
The latest veterinary medical news.

Activities

Canine Freestyle Federation
www.canine-freestyle.com
This site is devoted to canine freestyle—dancing with your dog. There's information about freestyle events, tips, and even music to choose!

Delta Society
www.deltasociety.org
The Delta Society promotes the human-animal bond through pet-assisted therapy and other programs.

Therapy Dogs International
www.tdi-dog.org
Therapy Dogs International certifies therapy dogs.

Travel

Dog Friendly
www.dogfriendly.com
Information about traveling with dogs, including guidebooks.

Travel Dog
www.traveldog.com
Lots of information on where you and your dog will be welcome when you travel.

Index

adoptions, rescue organizations, 45
adult dogs
 diet switching, 64
 housetraining introduction,
  126–128
 leash introduction, 112
 new home introduction, 54–56
 ownership pros/cons, 35, 37
 vaccine guidelines, 86–87
Advantage, spot-on flea preventative, 83
age, new home introduction, 43
American Animal Hospital Association
 (AHVA), 84, 86–87
American Kennel Club (AKC), 11–17,
 21–22
American Pet Products Manufacturers
 Association (APPMA), 52
American Veterinary Dental Society
 (AVDS), gum disease statistics, 78
anal glands, impacted, 93
anatomy, illustrated, 10
anesthesia sensitivity, 90
apartment dwellers, space savers, 26
appetite loss, health indicator, 95
Arizona Dogs, breed history, 22
ASPCA Animal Poison Control Center,
 101
Association of American Feed Control
 Officials (AAFCO), 58, 61
attention (focus), training, 120–122
automobiles, flea proofing, 81
Aztecs, breed history, 18, 19–10

baby gates, housetraining, 125
backyard breeders, avoiding, 41–42

bathrooms, 50
baths, grooming guidelines, 75–77
bedrooms, 50
behavior problems, 109–111
BioSpot, flea preventative, 72, 83
bladder stones, symptoms, 90
body, breed characteristics, 16
body language, 113, 131–132
bones, avoiding, 66
Bordetella bronchiseptica, 87
Borrelia burgdorferi (Lyme disease), 87
breed characteristics, 11–17, 25–26
breeders, 39–41, 45, 84
breed history, 18–22
breed standards, 11, 12–17
broken bones, 95
brushes, 71, 73
burn injury, 100

canine adenovirus-2, 86–87
canine distemper virus, 86–87
canine parainfluenza virus, 87
canine parvovirus, 86–87
canines, pack theory, 105–106
canned foods, 60
Capstar, systemic flea preventative, 83
chew toys, guidelines, 53
Chihuahua Club of America (CCA),
 12–17
Chihuahueno, breed history, 22
children, ownership, 29–30
chocolate, avoiding, 66
choking, 96
clickers, positive markers, 113–114
climate, chill concerns, 30–31

coats, 14, 27–28, 39, 71–73
cold weather, chill concerns, 30–31
collapsing trachea, 91
collars, 52–53, 111
colors, 28, 39
come command, training, 117–118
companionship, 24, 27–28
conditioner/shampoo, baths, 76
cooperation, training techniques, 123
core vaccines, guidelines, 86–87
costs, ownership responsibility, 24
crates, 53, 54, 127
cuts/scratches, treatment, 101

diarrhea, 97–98
dishes (food/water), 53
distemper-measles virus, 87
dogs (other household), supervision, 34
down command, training, 115–116
dry (kibble) foods, pros/cons, 59–60

ears, 16, 32, 77–78
ectropion, tear staining cause, 79–80
emergency care, 96–97, 99
enzymatic cleaners, housetraining, 126
equipment/supplies
    grooming, 70
    housetraining, 124–126
    purchasing guidelines, 52–54
    training, 111
exercise, minimal requirements, 28
exercise pens, housetraining, 126
external parasites, 71, 80–83
eyes, 15–16, 32, 79–80, 98

family, ownership responsibilities, 24
feeding schedules, 63–65
feet, nail trimming, 74–75
females, 38, 89
first-aid kits, 99
fleas/ticks, 71, 80–83
focus (attention), training, 120–122
fontanel. See molera
food dishes, guidelines, 53

foods
    AAFCO, 58, 61
    canned, 60
    diet formulas, 65
    diet switching, 64
    dry (kibble), 59–60
    homemade diets, 62–63
    label elements, 61
    picky eaters, 65–67
    quantity guidelines, 63–65
    semi-moist, 60
    supplements, 60
    treats, 60–62
    types to avoid, 66
    water, 67, 129
friends (guests), 33–34, 84
Frontline Plus, 72, 83

garages, 51
grooming
    baths, 75–77
    coats, 71–73
    ears, 77–78
    eye care, 79–80
    health observation opportunity, 71
    nail trimming, 74–75
    Smooths, 69–70
    supplies/equipment, 53, 70
    teeth care, 78–79
grooming table, 70
guarantees, responsible breeders, 45
guests (friends), cautious attitude, 33–34

hair dryers, bathing equipment, 76
handling, 44, 56
heads, breed characteristics, 15
health guarantee, 45
health problems. See individual problem
hearing sense, 32
heart disease, 91–92
heatstroke, 98–100
height/weight, breed characteristics, 13
holistic medicines, 85–86
homemade diets, 62–63

housetraining, 24–136
hydrocephalus, 92
hypoglycemia, 65, 92

impacted anal glands, 93
inappropriate behavior, remote punishment controls, 109–111
insect growth regulators (IGRs), 83
insect stings, 100–101
Internet, puppy source, 42

K-9 Advantix, flea preventative, 72, 83
kibble (dry) foods, 59–60
kitchens, 56, 128

leadership, canine pack theory, 105–106
leashes, 52–53, 111–113
leptospirosis, 87
let's go command, training, 119–120
life spans, breed traits, 29
life's rewards, positive reinforcement, 107
lifestyles, ownership, 23–25
Long Coats, 14, 27, 38, 71–73
Lyme disease (Borrelia burgdorferi), 87

males, 38, 89
Malta, breed development history, 20–21
mange, 82
Mayans, breed history, 18–19
Mediterranean region, history, 20–21
Mexican Chihuahuas, breed history, 22
Mexico, breed history, 18–20
mites, mange prevention/treatment, 82
molera, 15, 20, 22, 44, 93
mouth/tongue, 32, 78
movement, breed characteristics, 17

nail cutters, guidelines, 53
nails, trimming, 74–75
neuter/spay, health, 89
newspapers, 125, 128–129
noncore vaccines, guidelines, 86–87
noses, smelling sense, 32

OK command, training release, 115
ownership
    adult dog selection, 35, 37
    negative traits, 29–33
    puppy selection, 35, 36–37
    reasons for, 25–29
    responsibilities, 23–25, 57

pack theory, 105–106
pancreatitis, 93
patella luxation, 93–94
paws, touch sense, 32
Perro Chihuahueno, breed history, 19
pet stores, avoiding, 42–43
physical punishment, versus positive reinforcement, 107–111
picky eaters, diet guidelines, 65–67
plants, poisonous, 49, 51
plastic bags, housetraining supplies, 125
playful, breed characteristic, 28
pockets, size designation, 13, 45
poisoning, 101
poisonous plants, 49, 51
pooper scoopers, housetraining, 125
popularity rankings, 11, 22
positive markers, training, 113–114
positive reinforcement, versus physical punishment, 107–111
Program, systemic flea preventative, 83
puddle pads, housetraining supplies, 125
puppies
    diet switching, 64
    elimination behavior, 131–132
    first night guidelines, 55–56
    health indicators, 44
    housetraining, 126–128, 134–136
    hypoglycemia risks, 65
    leash introduction, 112
    locating, 39–43
    new home introduction, 43, 54–56
    ownership pros/cons, 35, 36–37
    selection criteria, 43–45
    vaccine guidelines, 86–87
puppy corrals, housetraining, 128–131

rabies, 86–87
recalls, training techniques, 118
relationships, canine pack, 105–106
remote punishment, 109–111
rescue organizations, 45
resources, 137–140
retained deciduous teeth, removal, 94
retractable leashes, avoiding, 52–53
Revolution, spot-on flea preventative, 83
rewards, 107, 113–114

schedules, 63–65, 134–136
scratches/cuts, treatment, 101
seeing sense, 32
semi-moist foods, 60
senses, canine abilities, 32
shampoo/conditioner, baths, 76
sit command, training, 114–115
size, breed characteristics, 13
slipping stiffles. *See* patella luxation
smelling sense, 32
Smooths, 14, 27, 38, 69–73
snoring, 31
snorting, 31, 33
socialization, training, 105–106
sounds, remote punishment, 110–111
space requirements, 26
spay/neuter, health considerations, 89
spot-ons (topical treatments), 83
spray (water) bottles, 110, 111
standards, breed, 11, 12
static electricity, nylon comb/brush, 71
stay command, training, 116–117
styptic powder/pencil, nail trimming, 75
supplements, 60
supplies. *See* equipment/supplies
systemic products, flea preventative, 83

tables, grooming, 70
taste sense, 32
teacups, size designation, 13, 45

tear staining, reasons for, 79–80
Techichi, breed history, 19
teeth, 78–79, 94
temperament, breed characteristics, 17
temperature, chill concerns, 30–31
tethers, training techniques, 112–113
Texas Dogs, breed history, 22
ticks, 71–72, 80–83
tinies, size designation, 13, 45
Toltecs, breed history, 18, 19
tongue/mouth, 32, 78
toothpaste/toothbrush, 78–79
topical treatments (spot-ons), 83
touch sense, 32
toys, 28, 53, 54, 111
training, 105–123
travel, ownership reason, 27–28
Treasure Hunt game, 121–122
treats, 60–62, 107, 113–114

UKC, breed standards, 12–17
United States, breed history, 21–22

vaccines, guidelines, 86–87
veterinarians, 56–57, 84–87, 96–97
vocalizations, 110–114

walks, exercise opportunity, 28
watchdogs, breed characteristic, 33–34
water, always available, 67, 129
water dishes, guidelines, 53
water (spray) bottles, 110, 111
Watson, James, breed history, 22
weather, chill concerns, 30–31
weight/height, breed characteristics, 13
whiskers, touch sense, 32

x-pens, housetraining equipment, 126

yards, 49, 51, 81, 128–129

Photo credits

Bonnie Nance: 1, 20, 23, 27, 30, 46-47, 62, 91, 95, 102-103, 130, 133; *Isabelle Francais:* 4-5, 8-9, 14, 19, 35, 36, 38, 52, 57, 59, 66, 70, 73, 74, 77, 79, 82, 84, 88, 90, 124, 128, 131; *Kent Dannen:* 11, 13, 16, 18, 25, 31, 33, 34, 40, 43, 48, 49, 55, 58, 63, 67, 68, 69, 78, 85, 92, 94, 98, 100, 104, 126, 134